FOOTBALL FACTS

WITHDRAWN

NOT TO BE TAKEN AWAY

FANTASTIC
FOOTBALL
FACTS

BY NICK CALLOW

First published in Great Britain in 2004 by
Virgin Books Ltd
Thames Wharf Studios
Rainville Road
London
W6 9HA

ISBN 07535 0987 3

Typeset by Phoenix Photosetting, Chatham, Kent
Printed and bound in Great Britain by Bookmarque Ltd

CONTENTS

CONTENTS

CONTENTS

FOREWORD

When you are presenting six hours of live football every Saturday it pays to get your facts straight. Trying to handle the likes of Rodney Marsh, George Best and Frank McLintock while a producer screams in my ear and a succession of results appear on a screen in front of me is distracting enough. Yet I still need to be alert enough to glance down at my notes and bring out a relevant fact or statistic ... and get it right!

Which on more than one occasion, I admit, I haven't. The most recent misplaced stat was when I insisted that no one had scored a penalty against Manchester United since 1993. I had forgotten York City's in a cup game two years later. Rodney hadn't and never fails to remind me that I got it wrong.

People always assume I have an army of researchers labouring away in a darkened room, spoonfeeding me all this information. The truth is I spend most of the week preparing for the show on my own, trying to learn as much as possible before we go on air.

This book will definitely become an essential part of my weekly routine. It contains a wealth of fascinating and obscure bits of information and I look forward to throwing a few trivia questions out to the panel this season. I might even stump Rodney!

Jeff Stelling

SUPER SUBS

These days football managers are paid a very good salary to train the players and pick the team. But never do they earn their money more than with the inspired substitutions that change the face of the game...

David Fairclough – Liverpool v St Etienne, 1977
The flame-haired winger was the original 'super-sub' after his exploits at Liverpool. His finest hour was undoubtedly coming off the bench to score the winner in the second leg of the European Cup quarter-final against St Etienne. Liverpool had lost the first leg 1–0 in France and looked set to crash out on away goals with the score standing at 2–1 at Anfield with less than ten minutes remaining.

Reds boss Bob Paisley took the brave decision to bring off powerful striker John Toshack for pacy wide-man Fairclough and the move paid dividends almost immediately.

On 84 minutes Fairclough burst through on the left and rifled his shot into the corner of the net to the delight of most of the 55,043 packed into the ground. The goal proved vital as Liverpool went on to lift the European Cup.

Fairclough eventually scored 18 goals after coming on for Liverpool as a sub – a club record – but also scored 37 times as a starter.

Karl-Heinz Rummenigge – Germany v France, 1982
This World Cup semi-final is most memorable for Harald Schumacher's outrageous assault on Patrick Battison. But

FANTASTIC FOOTBALL FACTS

Rummenigge came off the bench with Germany 3–1 down in extra time to pull one back and then inspire his team to level and take the game into a shoot-out, where he subsequently scored the decisive penalty!

Ian Wright – Crystal Palace v Manchester United, 1990
Having only recently recovered from a broken leg, Wright came on for Crystal Palace who were 2–1 down with only 20 minutes left in the FA Cup final. The striker received the ball from Mark Bright and conjured up an equaliser. He scored again to put the Eagles ahead in extra time, but United pulled level and eventually won the replay.

Gianfranco Zola – Chelsea v VfB Stuttgart, 1998
The Italian footballing genius scored a sensational goal just 19 seconds after coming on in the Cup-Winners' Cup final to win the trophy for the Blues.

Teddy Sheringham – Manchester United v Newcastle United, 1999
Sheringham came off the bench as a replacement for the injured Roy Keane and it proved a decisive move with Teddy opening the scoring almost immediately, as United went on to win 2–0.

Ole Gunnar Solskjaer – Manchester United v Bayern Munich, 1999
The baby-faced assassin's finest hour came in the Champions League final when he came on in the 81st-minute to net the last-gasp winner in added time that capped a remarkable turnaround by United and secured their amazing Treble success.

Savo Milosevic – Yugoslavia v Slovenia, 2000
The much-maligned former Aston Villa striker proved his side's saviour in the European Championships. At 3–0 down, and playing with ten men, Savo came off the bench to turn the tide with a well-taken brace as the Slavs went on to gain a draw and an important point in their group.

Niall Quinn – Republic of Ireland v Germany, 2002
During a World Cup group game, Ireland boss Mick McCarthy introduced the veteran striker with 17 minutes remaining. Appropriately it was Quinn who got the vital knockdown from Steve Finnan's long ball to allow Robbie Keane to burst through and score a precious late equaliser.

Wayne Rooney – Everton v Portsmouth, Leicester City, Birmingham City, 2003
The precocious youngster was best used as a reserve by David Moyes during this spell. He scored three in four games, all of which he had started on the bench.

NOT SO SUPER SUBS
Unfortunately it can also go horribly wrong. Here are some substitutes who had a day to forget.

John Ritchie, 1972
The Stoke City player became one of the fastest dismissals as a substitute when he was sent off in a UEFA Cup tie against Kaiserslautern. Ritchie was red-carded just 40 seconds after entering the field.

Alan Smith, 1992
Gary Lineker's international career came to a frustrating end at the European Championships in Sweden. With the striker a single goal behind Bobby Charlton's England scoring record of 49, England were drawing 1–1 with the hosts when Lineker was substituted after just 61 minutes and Arsenal's Alan Smith ran on in his place. England went on to lose 2–1 and Lineker had made his last appearance for his country. Surprisingly Smith never did follow in Lineker's footsteps!

FANTASTIC FOOTBALL FACTS

Marco Etcheverry, 1994
Bolivian midfielder Marco Etcheverry suffered an embarrassing international appearance against Germany in June 1994, being sent off just three minutes after coming on as a second half-substitute.

Gianfranco Zola, 1994
During the World Cup at USA '94 Italian forward Gianfranco Zola was left in shock as he was dismissed on 78 minutes – just 12 minutes after coming on as a substitute. Zola discovered he could play no further part in the tournament – and to add to his misery the incident took place on his 28th birthday!

Patrick Suffo, 2002
Cameroon striker Patrick Suffo endured a nightmare in an international against Germany.

Suffo was brought on as a substitute on 53 minutes, but was sent off 23 minutes later following two yellow cards. Moments later Miroslav Klose scored to wrap up a 2–0 win for the Germans.

Marco Zwyssig, 2003
In the second leg of a UEFA Cup match Basel needed to beat Newcastle by two clear goals to win the tie. However, Marco Zwyssig was injured after just 16 seconds and young defender Boris Smiljanic was brought on to replace him on the five-minute mark.

Smiljanic was supposed to plug the defence, but ten minutes later he as good as ended his side's chances of turning the tide with a nightmarish own goal.

GREAT DEBUTS

Most players' debuts are mundane affairs. For a few, however, they bring a glut of goals or come in a glamorous cup final.

Jim Dyet scored eight goals on his debut for King's Park in their 12–2 win over Forfar in a Scottish Division 2 game in January 1930.

Len Shackleton, signed in the week from Bradford Park Avenue, hit the target six times for Newcastle, who beat Newport County 13–0 in Division 2 in October 1946.

Henry Morris, of East Fife, scored a hat-trick on his Scotland debut – an 8–2 win over Northern Ireland in Belfast in October 1949. It was to prove his only international cap.

Alan Davies made his FA Cup debut for Manchester United in the 1983 Final against Brighton, playing in both the 2–2 draw and United's 4–0 success in the replay.

Alan Shearer, then 17, netted a hat-trick on his full debut for Southampton in a 4–2 win over Arsenal in Division 1 in April 1988.

Fabrizio Ravanelli paid off a chunk of his £7m transfer fee from Juventus with a hat-trick in his first Premiership match for Middlesbrough – a 3–3 draw against Liverpool in August 1996.

Stan Collymore, attempting to resurrect his Premiership career after leaving Aston Villa, scored three times on his home debut for Leicester – a 5–2 victory over Sunderland in March 2000.

Paulo Wanchope, a £3.65m summer signing from West Ham, scored three times on his home debut for Manchester City in a 4–2 win over Sunderland in August 2000.

David Ferrere, signed from French side Louhans, made his debut as a second-half substitute for Motherwell and scored a hat-trick in their 4–0 Scottish Premier League win over Hibernian in February 2002.

Jermaine Pennant marked his full Premiership debut for Arsenal with three goals against Southampton in May 2003 – Robert Pires scored the other three in a 6–1 'dress rehearsal' victory for the FA Cup final.

Queen's Park newcomer Steve Reilly netted a hat-trick of penalties on his home debut – a 5–2 win over Elgin City in the Scottish Division 3 in August 2003.

New manager Bobby Williamson saw Plymouth clinch the Division 2 championship with a 2–0 win over QPR in April 2004 in his first match in charge at Home Park after leaving Hibernian to take over from Paul Sturrock.

AWFUL DEBUTS
Putting a new player into a team is supposed to improve things and give the fans a lift in the hope that maybe results might just improve enough to get some glory or safety. But for many players what should be a special day can turn into a nightmare.

Reginald Williamson
The Middlesbrough keeper has the not so impressive claim of being the only England player to score an own goal on debut. Ireland were the beneficiaries in a 1–1 draw way, way back in 1905.

Steve Bruce
He was more of a loser than a winner for Manchester United despite their 2–1 win over Portsmouth in December 1987. He broke his nose, gave away a penalty and was booked in his first appearance for the club.

Ali Dia
Dia had convinced Southampton boss Graeme Souness that he was the cousin of AC Milan star George Weah and got a place on the bench against Leeds in November 1996. But Souness saw no family

resemblance in the 2–0 defeat and subbed the substitute within 55 minutes of him coming on. Dia was next seen trying his luck with non-League Gateshead.

Jason Crowe

This defender had nothing to laugh about when he came off the bench to make his Arsenal debut in a League Cup tie against Birmingham in October 1997. Crowe was shown the red card after just 33 seconds on the pitch and entered the record books for the wrong reasons. It didn't cost Arsenal the match though, as they cruised through 4–1.

Rio Ferdinand

After joining Leeds for a British record £18m from West Ham, Ferdinand was made to look a terrible waste of money at Leicester in December 2000. Leeds were three goals down inside half an hour as Ferdinand's presence caused confusion and calamity among his new team-mates and left Mark Viduka's late goal a mere consolation.

Richard Wright

The highly rated keeper was given a chance to impress before Euro 2000 when handed his first start for England in a friendly against Malta, but he conceded two penalties and scored an own goal in England's 2–1 win. Wright earned some credit by saving the second spot kick, but not enough to get a game in the Championships.

Rigobert Song

West Ham turned to the Cameroon international after selling Ferdinand to Leeds, quickly buying him in time to play in a League Cup tie against Sheffield Wednesday in December 2000. Song was terribly off key and missed his notes as he slipped to let Owen Morrison score an easy goal and the home side went on to lose 2–1 at Upton Park.

FANTASTIC FOOTBALL FACTS

Jose Antonio Reyes

At some £20m, Reyes became Arsenal's record transfer signing in January 2004. The former Seville striker proved his finishing prowess on his first start when he found the bottom corner of the net in the League Cup semi-final against Middlesbrough, but it was past his own goalkeeper and the resulting 2–1 defeat ensured Arsenal were out of the competition.

BIZARRE MERCHANDISE

These days replica kits and merchandising provide an essentially lucrative source of income for clubs of all levels and have even been rumoured to influence the selection of transfer targets – just think how much Bolton Wanderers made every time somebody had Giannakopoulos printed on the back of their shirt!

But what started as a simple scarf knitted in your team's colours has now become a seemingly endless, desperate and at times taste-less quest to stamp the club's corporate logo onto an ever-increasing number of goods.

At Chelsea's 'Megastore' you can uncover a selection of seductive offerings, including a monogrammed ladies' garter and a three-pack of thongs, ideal for those who've scored – cheeky!

Newcastle United supporters suck? At least the very young ones do according to 'NUFC Direct' who tempt parents with baby 'soothers' or a bag of sweets.

To help with spills, possibly caused when supporters leap up off the sofa while watching the game, Aston Villa offer a pack of three tea towels. Alternatively, in true Sunday newspaper colour-supplement style, a bone-china thimble and bell.

Displaying all the finesse of club owner Mohammed Al Fayed's other retail outlets, 'Fulham Today' customers can procure an attractive beach-inflatable shaped like the club's badge.

Middlesbrough clearly have inside knowledge and, within the 'What The Fans Want' section of their MFC Direct catalogue, provide fans with the opportunity to purchase a dog harness or dominoes set.

Not content with bumper stickers and air fresheners shaped like a football shirt, 'Saints Shop' customers can customise their vehicles, starting with a Southampton FC car mat set.

In the close season Portsmouth fans can turn their attention to an alternative hobby, thanks to 'Pompey Sport' stamp collections.

Breakfast is the most important meal of the day, a message not lost on 'Rover The Moon', Blackburn's online store – monogrammed egg-cup set anyone?

Spurs supporters can swot up for their local pub quiz and check exactly when Tottenham last won the League thanks to the leather-bound encyclopaedia on sale on the club website.

Intending to ensure everyone stays afloat, Everton's 'megastore' can provide Toffee-branded inflatable armbands.

And, thanks to Wolves, a commemorative brick – from your favourite stand at Molineux.

SUPERSTITIONS

Footballers are a funny bunch, and some of them take bizarre behaviour to new levels with their superstitions...

Chelsea skipper John Terry could fill this section on his own for he really is a tortured soul with a bizarre pre-match routine for home games. Even he describes the following as 'ridiculous':

- Refusing any sort of drink until after kick off

FANTASTIC FOOTBALL FACTS

- Only using toilets to the right of the changing rooms

- Counting all the lampposts on his journey to Stamford Bridge

He also has a problem with shirt numbers and explains: 'I was offered the chance to be Chelsea's No. 5, but I am a superstitious person and just felt it would be wrong. My number at the club is 26. So that's why I keep it.'

Then there are other pre-match problems. He adds: 'It's stupid things like always rotating tape round my shin-pads three times and never going to the two toilets on the left of the dressing room.'

Former England midfielder Paul Ince has stuck to his pre-match superstition for as long as he can remember. It involves always being the last player running out, holding his shirt in his hands, which he only puts on as he goes onto the pitch.

Former Tottenham and Chelsea defender Jason Cundy was once quoted as saying: 'I always kiss my ring before a match.' Now there's a feat.

Millwall chairman Theo Paphitis might have had a couple of empty seats alongside him at the 2004 FA Cup final against Manchester United as he had a thing about wearing the same old lucky suit during his team's Cup run. He joked in the build up: 'I've got to get my clothes clean, but I can't now.'

Derby County once feared their lack of success in the FA Cup was due to reports that their former Baseball Ground was built on a gypsy camping ground. Prior to the 1946 final, Derby County players went so far as to ask the gypsies to lift the curse ... and the plan worked as they beat Charlton Athletic.

France captain Lauren Blanc would always kiss the bald head of his goalkeeping team-mate Fabien Barthez before a match on their way to winning the World Cup in 1998. After Blanc was suspended for the final he still kissed the keeper's head, at the side of the pitch, wearing his suit.

Arsenal defender Lee Dixon was also suited and booted when he kept a superstition going with team-mate Kevin Campbell in a game against Norwich. The Gunners duo had a routine which involved Dixon always running out before Campbell, only this time with Dixon injured he dashed down from the stands before kick-off to keep his side of the bargain.

In Argentina, there was a goalkeeper, Sergio Goycochea, who used to urinate on the pitch every time there was a penalty. He started doing this in the semi-final of the World Cup in Italy in 1990 and it worked, so he kept doing it all the time.

Still in South America, Rosario Central manager Edgardo Bauza always wore the same jacket, game after game, even in the sweltering heat of the summer.

'I think everyone has a lucky item, even if they don't make a show of it. But the teams have another kind of superstition. For example my team, Rosario, once brought a witch to the stadium to protect their goal line. Racing, a team from Buenos Aires, even organised a huge pilgrimage in 1998, with priests and everything, to change their luck,' explains Bauza.

And there are also rituals to bring bad luck to opponents. For example, Racing fans bring lots of sugar to throw onto the pitch when they play against Independiente (another team from Buenos Aires). Boca fans used to bring chickens into the stadium when they played against River Plate (it's now forbidden).

EVEN THE PRESIDENT GETS INVOLVED

'The funniest superstition involves our ex-president, Carlos Menem,' explains Rosario Central fan Sergio Rinaldi. 'There's a tradition that Mr Menem – during the ten years that he was in power – brought bad luck to the country. He's a fan of River Plate, so the opposing side is always happy when he comes to watch his team play.

On one occasion, San Lorenzo supporters brought a huge picture of Mr Menem when their team played against River Plate. The former president wasn't there, but he apparently worked his magic and San Lorenzo romped home to victory.

Arsenal goalkeepers refuse to wear a new shirt unless it has been washed – a superstition that dates back to the 1927 FA Cup final. The Gunners went down 1–0 to Cardiff City, and Dan Lewis, the keeper, blamed the goal that led to defeat on his 'slippery new jersey'.

The German midfielder Christian Ziege always plays wearing a T-shirt with a picture of his son printed on it, under his team shirt.

One of the stars of the 1998 World Cup, Mexican striker Luis Fernandez always wears an amulet, containing a photo of his daughter.

Having worn the same tie for every game while managing Argentina during their World Cup triumph in 1986, Carlos Salvador Bilardo then wore his 'lucky' neckwear with less effect at the 1990 Finals.

The Portsmouth outside right Fred Worrall was a very superstitious player. For the 1939 FA Cup final, he allegedly took as many 'lucky' tokens as he could find onto the pitch with him: a small horseshoe in his pocket; a sprig of white heather pushed down each of his socks; and a small white elephant fastened to one of his tie-ups. Fred might have been slightly weighed down, but Pompey still won the final 4–1 against Wolverhampton Wanderers.

CHANGING PLACES

Wearing the shirt of your country is the highest honour possible for most professional footballers. However, some players have managed to represent two different countries during their careers. Whether or not they succeeded in learning the words to both national anthems is unclear!

The legendary Alfredo di Stefano actually played international football for THREE different countries during his illustrious career.

Born in Buenos Aires in 1926, the striker represented Argentina seven times and scored seven goals.

In 1949, due to a players' strike in his homeland, di Stefano opted to move to Colombia, where clubs were prepared to pay huge salaries to star players and played four games for the national side – although these matches are not recognised by FIFA.

Four years later, the prolific goalscorer moved to Real Madrid and was able to represent Spain 31 times, scoring 23 goals in the process.

Ladislao Kubala matched this amazing feat by also playing for three nations between 1946 and 1961.

He made his international debut for Czechoslovakia at the age of 19, but six games later he turned out for Hungary.

Kubala won just three caps for the Hungarians before switching nationalities again to represent Spain after his move to Barcelona, scoring 11 goals in 19 games.

Ferenc Puskas was yet another Spanish international of the 1960s who had previously played for another country. The forward represented his native Hungary before the uprising in 1956 which led to his exile from his homeland.

More recently, Ryan Giggs turned out for England Schoolboys – indeed captained the side – before becoming the wing wizard for Wales.

FANTASTIC FOOTBALL FACTS

However, he refutes suggestions that he could have worn the Three Lions at full international level. 'People saying I should have played for England makes me furious. I am one hundred per cent Welsh and did not chose Wales – I had no choice,' he explains.

Former Arsenal goalkeeper Bob Wilson also played for England Schoolboys without then going on to represent the senior side.

Wilson, born in Chesterfield, played with Nobby Stiles in the 1957 schoolboys side, but was eligible to represent Scotland at full international level via family ancestry and won two caps.

Australian midfielder Tim Cahill spent nine years fighting a FIFA ruling which prevented him from playing for his country of birth.

Cahill had previously played for Western Samoa in an Under-20 tournament while on a family holiday, even though he featured for just five minutes and was only 14 at the time.

FIFA refused to allow him to play for the Socceroos until 2004 when the rules were changed to discount appearances at Under-21 level and below.

Stan Mortensen was an England star who scored 23 goals in 25 appearances for his country.

However, his international debut came in bizarre circumstances for Wales against England in a wartime clash at Wembley in 1943.

Mortensen was a reserve for England as Welshman Ivor Powell suffered an injury, but the English sportingly allowed their man to come on as a sub.

Wales were 4–1 down at the time and Mortensen ended up losing, or should that be winning, the match 8–3.

England hero Bobby Moore lifted the World Cup as captain in 1966 and won 108 caps.

But he also later skippered Team America against England during the Bicentennial Cup tournament in 1976 while playing for San Antonio Thunder in the North American Soccer League.

COLLECTORS' CORNER

Many football fans while away the hours bidding for old shirts, tickets and programmes on websites such as E-bay, but major auction houses have brought out the big-money buyers in pursuit of medals, shirts and trophies won by some of the game's biggest names.

£1.8m – Bobby Moore's collection of trophies and medals was bought by West Ham in June 2000. They included Moore's England World Cup-winners' medal.

£274,410 – The proceeds from 129 lots put up for sale by Sir Geoff Hurst in September 2000. They included his England World Cup-winning shirt (£91,750), his cap (£37,600) and his Man of the Match trophy (£18,800). A donation went to the Bobby Moore Imperial Cancer Research Fund.

£157,750 – The No. 10 shirt worn by Pele in Brazil's 1970 World Cup victory was snapped up by an anonymous bidder in March 2002.

£150,000 – Sir Geoff Hurst's England World Cup-winners' medal was acquired by West Ham in August 2001.

£124,750 – Gordon Banks's 1966 England World Cup-winners' medal went to an anonymous bidder in March 2001.

£100,000 – Caps, medals and other memorabilia from the career of Billy Wright, the first England player to appear in 100 internationals, were in demand when sold in November 1996.

£88,000 – Trophies, caps and medals won by former Arsenal and Liverpool player Ray Kennedy fetched this sum in October 1993.

£80,000 – The total raised by honours won by England's successful World Cup manager Sir Alf Ramsey. Tottenham and Ipswich, two of his clubs, were among the buyers.

FANTASTIC FOOTBALL FACTS

SHOW US YOUR MEDALS
When the pub debates break out with regards to who is ultimately the best footballer, there is only one objective way of ending the argument – what did they win?

25 – Pele (Santos, New York Cosmos, Brazil)
Three World Cups, eleven Sao Paulo State Championships, six Brazilian Cups, two Copa Libertadores, two World Club Championships and one USA Championship.

24 – Kenny Dalglish (Celtic, Liverpool)
The striker claimed 24 medals as a player made up of six Scottish championship titles, two Scottish FA Cups, seven English League titles, four League Cups, one FA Cup, three European Cups and one European Super Cup. He also picked up two Footballer of the Year awards and won two more English League titles as a manager with Liverpool and Blackburn Rovers.

22 – Ally McCoist (Glasgow Rangers)
McCoist won his amazing collection of medals thanks to ten Scottish League titles, three Scottish Cups and nine Scottish League Cups.

21 – Paolo Maldini (AC Milan)
Seven Serie A titles, two Intercontinental Cups, four European Super Cups, one Italian Cup, two European Cups, two Champions League titles and three Italian Super Cups.

17 – Phil Neal (Liverpool)
Seven English League titles, four League Cups, four European Cups, one UEFA Cup and one European Super Cup.

16 – Alan Hansen (Liverpool)
The defender picked up 16 honours made up of 8 English League titles, three League Cups, two FA Cups and three European Cups.

15 – Denis Irwin (Manchester United)
Seven Premiership titles, three FA Cups, one League Cup, one European Cup, one European Cup-Winners' Cup, one European Super Cup and one Intercontinental Cup.

15 – Ian Rush (Liverpool)
Five English League titles, three FA Cups, one European Cup, five League Cups and one famous Screen Sport Super Cup. Also awarded an MBE.

14 – Ryan Giggs (Manchester United)
Eight English League titles, three FA Cups, one Champions League, one Intercontinental Cup and one League Cup.

11 – Mark Hughes (Manchester United, Chelsea)
The Welshman won eleven honours, made up of four FA Cups, two European Cup-Winners' Cups, one European Super Cup, two League Cups and two English Premier League titles.

10 – Zinedine Zidane (Juventus, Real Madrid, France)
One World Cup, one European Championship, one Champions League, two Serie A titles, two European Super Cups, two World Club Cups and one La Liga title. Also claimed four individual honours as European Player of the year and three as World Player of the Year.

10 – Tony Adams (Arsenal)
Picked up his medals thanks to two English Premier League titles, two English League championships, three FA Cups, two League Cups and one European Cup-Winners' Cup.

WHAT A MISS

The striker dances his way past the goalkeeper, the fans are already celebrating and the manager has already leaped out of his dug-out. But things can still go horribly wrong. Remember these world-class howlers when a goal seemed an absolute certainty?

Billy Bremner
The midfielder could – and probably should – have burned his name into Scottish football folklore by scoring the goal that would have knocked Brazil out of the World Cup in 1974.

But Bremner failed to react quickly enough as the ball came back off the post, Scotland had to settle for a 0–0 draw and ultimately finished behind Brazil in the group on goal difference.

Kevin Keegan
England pummelled Spain looking for the goals that would have put them through to the 1982 World Cup semi-final. With only a few minutes remaining the golden chance fell to star striker Kevin Keegan, but his flicked header sent the ball wide from just six yards. Maybe the shaggy perm got in the way.

Gordon Smith
Unfancied Brighton were tied 2–2 with mighty Manchester United in the last minute of extra time in the FA Cup final of 1983 when Smith was found free in the area. It was such a clear chance that even the commentator said 'And Smith must score', but his shot was saved easily by Gary Bailey, a fanzine was born and United went on to win the replay 4–0.

FANTASTIC FOOTBALL FACTS

Geoff Thomas
The Crystal Palace midfielder's England career was ruined with one missed chance in a friendly against France in 1992. Thomas tried an audacious chip when put through, but sadly it barely got off the ground and ended up closer to the corner flag and the fans never forgave him despite a 2–0 victory.

Ronnie Rosenthal
Rosenthal set the benchmark for bad misses while playing for Liverpool against Aston Villa in 1993 when he struck the bar rather the empty net from just ten yards. Liverpool's 4–2 defeat just added salt into the Israeli striker's wounds.

Andy Cole
Cole was guilty of more than one crucial miss in the 1–1 draw at West Ham in 1995 and it cost Manchester United the championship. Rivals Blackburn were losing at Liverpool, but United still had to win at Upton Park. In the last ten minutes Cole was put through time and time again, but he failed to beat Ludek Miklosko and the trophy went to Rovers.

Paul Gascoigne
Gazza was never the fastest of players once he discovered what delights were on offer off the pitch and his lack of pace was to haunt him in the semi-final of Euro '96 against Germany. The midfielder had an open goal to aim at as he slid in to convert Darren Anderton's pass, but he missed the ball completely and England eventually went out on penalties.

Christian Vieri
Italy blamed the match officials for their shock 2–1 defeat to South Korea in the 2002 World Cup, but they should have pointed the finger at Vieri. The striker, who cost Inter Milan £32m, skied the ball

over an open goal from two yards out with a minute left and Italy lost the game in extra time.

Ryan Giggs
Four years after knocking Arsenal out of the FA Cup with a wonder goal, the Manchester United winger tried to repeat his heroics only to suffer humiliation. Once again he dribbled around the Arsenal defence, but somehow chipped the ball over an unguarded net and United lost 2–0.

THE KEEPER HAS SCORED!
They are only supposed to stop goals, but sometimes goalkeepers become heroes at the other end. Whether it's a lucky long punt upfield or a dramatic last-gasp effort with everything at stake – these keepers managed to get their names on the scoresheet.

Blackburn's American international Brad Friedel came up for a last-minute corner and scored an equaliser against Charlton in February 2004. However, Friedel then managed to let another goal in at the other end and Charlton won the match.

Peter Schmeichel, who headed an 89th-minute equaliser for Manchester United in a 1995 UEFA Cup tie, became the first keeper to score in the Premiership when he volleyed in for Aston Villa in a 3–2 defeat by Everton in October 2001.

Notts County keeper Steve Mildenhall scored the winner with a free kick from inside his own half in the August 2001 League Cup first-round tie against Mansfield Town and their goalie Kevin Pilkington.

Mark Bosnich scored with a penalty when Australia beat the Solomon Islands 13–0 in a World Cup qualifier in June 2001.

Jimmy Glass scored a last-minute winner in Carlisle's 2–1 win over Plymouth in May 1999. In doing so, Glass, on loan from Swindon,

FANTASTIC FOOTBALL FACTS

kept Carlisle in the Football League and sent Scarborough into non-League football.

In November 1999, Paraguay's Jose Luis Chilavert scored a hat-trick of penalties in Velez Sarsfield's 6–1 win over Ferro Carril Oeste in the Argentine League.

Chesterfield's Arthur Birch holds the record for most goals by a keeper in a season thanks to his five penalties in Division Three North in 1923–24.

GOALS FROM GOAL KICKS

Chris Mackenzie for Hereford against Barnet's Maik Taylor in a Third Division match in August 1995.

Iain Hesford scored the winner for Maidstone in their 3–2 Fourth Division clash with Hereford and their keeper Tony Elliott in November 1991.

East Fife's Ray Charles beat Stranraer's Bernard Duffy in a Scottish Division Two match in February 1990.

The Irish League Cup final was won by Glentoran's Alan Patterson, who hit an 87th-minute goal kick to beat Linfield's George Dunlop and secure a 2–1 victory.

Dunlop had already been a goalkeeping victim in August 1998 when Andy McLean marked his Irish League debut with a long, long goal for Cliftonville.

In Scotland, Andy Goram scored for Hibs against Morton's Dave Wylie in a Premier Division match in 1988.

Coventry's Steve Ogrizovic scored in the English First Division in October 1986 against Martin Hodge of Sheffield Wednesday.

Two years before that Coventry's Raddy Avramovic conceded a goal to Watford shot stopper Steve Sherwood, also in the First Division.

Another keeper to score with a goal kick was Bristol City's Ray Cashley in a Second Division match against Jeff Wealands of Hull City. That came in September 1973.

The legendary Peter Shilton was playing in a First Division match for Leicester City in October 1967 when he scored against Southampton keeper Campbell Forsyth.

Irish giant and Tottenham keeper Pat Jennings beat Manchester United's Alex Stepney with a long punt in the 1967 FA Charity Shield.

JEEPERS KEEPERS

Goalkeepers have got so good at being bad that they are regularly appearing in videos showing their ineptitude. It is not quite so funny, however, if it is your keeper that has made the mistake which costs the team the game.

Ray Clemence

Few gaffes compare with the one committed by England keeper Clemence in 1976. Clem seemed to almost help the ball over the line as he bent down to save a weak shot by future Liverpool team-mate Kenny Dalglish and hand Scotland a memorable 2–1 win at Hampden Park.

Rene Higuita

Colombia were losing 1–0 to Cameroon in the second round game at World Cup '90 when the keeper tried to show his skills outside the area. Roger Milla tackled him with ease, though, and rolled the ball into the vacant net. It meant Colombia's late goal was not enough to avoid a 2–1 defeat.

FANTASTIC FOOTBALL FACTS

David Seaman
The ex-Arsenal keeper looked out of his depth when the Real Zaragoza midfielder Nayim lobbed him from the halfway line in the last minute of extra time to win the European Cup-Winners' Cup final 2–1 in 1995.

Tim Flowers
Then at Blackburn, Flowers was bamboozled as if facing a Shane Warne leg break in February 1996 when Liverpool striker Stan Collymore's gentle shot from 25 yards bounced in off his shoulder. It was to prove costly as Blackburn lost 3–2.

Shay Given
The Newcastle keeper was left embarrassed after losing track of Dion Dublin in a 2–2 draw with Coventry in November 1997. Given rolled the ball out to kick it up field only for the Coventry striker to run from behind him and put the ball in the empty net.

Peter Schmeichel
The Manchester United keeper proved that even the best can look the worst when, in the FA Cup Fifth Round in 1998, he sliced an attempted clearance and John Hendrie was able to just tap the ball home to give Barnsley the lead. Manchester United escaped with a 1–1 draw, but lost the replay 3–2.

Massimo Taibi
The Italian took over from legendary keeper Peter Schmeichel at Manchester United, but his career at Old Trafford soon went downhill after letting a tame 30-yard shot from Southampton's Matt Le Tissier go through his legs on his debut in September 1999. The game ended 3–3.

David Seaman
England had Seaman to thank for losing 2–1 to Brazil in the World

Cup quarter-final ,in June 2002. Spunky allowed Ronaldinho's cross
from a 40-yard free kick to drift over his head and into the top corner of the net.

Jerzy Dudek
Diego Forlan couldn't believe his luck in December 2002 when
Dudek let a simple headed back pass from Jamie Carragher
through his legs – the United hit man striking the ball into the empty
Liverpool goal. Liverpool never really recovered and lost 2-1.

Carlo Cudicini
Chelsea looked set for a rare point away to Arsenal in the 2003–04
season until Cudicini somehow let a weak Robert Pires cross
through his legs allowing the ball to bounce off Thierry Henry and
trickle over the line to seal a 2-1 defeat.

HOW DID HE GET THAT IN?
No matter how long a team's defence practises on the training
ground, there are some things you can't prepare for on a match day.
Being a manager in football can be stressful enough without seeing
all your hard work undone by freak goals such as these.

Jason Cundy, v Ipswich, 1992
The Tottenham defender was only trying to win a tackle 40 yards out,
but such was his clean contact on the ball, it flew into the top corner. Not bad for his first goal for the club and it earned his side a
point in a 1-1 draw.

Alan Hudson, v Ipswich, 1970
Chelsea couldn't believe their luck when referee Capey awarded
them a goal after Hudson's 20-yard shot hit a stanchion behind the
net. Capey thought the ball had gone through a hole in the side

netting after crossing the line. Ipswich failed to see the funny side as they lost 2–1.

Steve Livingstone, v Leicester, 1997
Arguably this was one of the most painful goals in history and not just because it helped Division 2 side Grimsby knock Premiership Leicester out of the League Cup 3–1. Leicester keeper Kasey Keller accidentally knocked out his own defender Julian Watts while trying to collect a long cross. Livingstone made the most of the mayhem to roll the ball towards goal and Steve Walsh ran back to clear the ball off the line, only to miss it and crack three ribs on the goalpost.

Dean Saunders, v Port Vale, 1998
The Sheffield United striker used all his cheek to help his side to a last-minute 2–1 victory. Vale keeper Paul Musselwhite ran out of his area to slide the ball out for a throw-in, but Saunders was there to take the throw quickly. He bounced the ball off Musselwhite's back and curled the rebound into the empty net.

Nayim, v Arsenal, 1995
A fluke or a flash of genius, it is still probably the most extraordinary goal to win a major trophy in European history. Real Zaragoza were level 1–1 with seconds left on the clock of the European Cup-Winners' Cup final when Nayim let fly from a full 50 yards.

The ball just eluded the desperate clutches of Arsenal keeper David Seaman and no one was sure whether the former Tottenham midfielder meant it or not.

Gary Sprake, v Liverpool, 1967
Leeds were in no danger when keeper Sprake chose to throw the ball out to team-mate Willie Bell. But he changed his mind as he began to let go and only succeeded in throwing the ball into his own net. There was no way back and they lost 2–0.

Marcus Browning, v Brentford, 1996
Brentford keeper Kevin Dearden was about to clear the ball when he heard a whistle and promptly dropped it in space. He thought it had come from the referee, but it was from a fan in the crowd and Bristol Rovers midfielder Browning scored into an empty net. Rovers won the game 2–1.

Peter Enckelman, v Birmingham, 2002
Birmingham had Enckelman and referee David Elleray to thank on the way to a 3–0 win over their fierce rivals. Villa defender Olof Mellberg threw the ball back to his keeper from a throw-in, but Enckelman somehow let the ball go under his foot and into the net. No team can score direct from a throw-in, but Elleray believed Enckelman clipped the ball on the way through and awarded a goal.

Artim Sakiri, v England, 2002
David Seaman won the last of his 75 England caps against Macedonia and it was easy to see why. Sakiri gave Macedonia a shock lead when Seaman allowed the midfielder's corner to go over his head and into the goal. England ended up drawing the European Championship qualifier 2–2.

Andy Gray, v Nottingham Forest, 1980
Forest lost the chance to win the League Cup for a third year in a row when keeper Peter Shilton collided with his own team-mate, defender David Needham. The ball ran to Wolves' Andy Gray and he scored into an empty net.

BAD HAIR DAY
Footballers have traditionally been style icons for teenagers to follow, but being on the cutting edge of style has left behind some casualties. Here are some of the more toe-curlingly cringeworthy examples.

FANTASTIC FOOTBALL FACTS

Bobby Charlton
The undisputed king of the comb-over. It seems that everybody, except Sir Bobby thought that he should have just gone bald gracefully rather than clinging on grimly to the wreckage of his hair.

Peter Beardsley
Every school had one kid who's mum thought it was acceptable to place a pudding bowl on their child's head and roughly cut around the edge. Well it seems that in Peter's house the trend never stopped.

Chris Waddle
The 80s pin-up sported a classic short on top, long on the side, mullet. Waddle took the mullet to a new level when he appeared on *Top of the Pops* crooning with Glenn Hoddle, but the low quality of the song deflected the abuse away from his hair.

Carlos Valderrama
The Colombian World Cup hero was instantly recognisable with his shock of blonde hair that made Don King seem conservative in his hair sense.

Trifon Ivanov
The defender was one of the more noticeable players for Bulgaria in the '94 World Cup because he just looked distinctly Eastern European. With his unkempt beard and shaggy hair he bore an uncanny resemblance to Baldrick from the TV comedy show *Blackadder*.

David Beckham
The housewives' favourite has a history of appalling hair cuts, such as the braids he had to meet Nelson Mandela. By far the worst had to be the Mr T Mohican style – let's just hope it is the Last of the Mohicans!

Paul Gascoigne
When Gazza first moved to Lazio he thought it was a good idea to have platinum blonde hair extensions – shame no one else did.

Ivan Campo
His long, curly mop of black greasy hair makes him look more like a singer in a funk band than a defensive hardman.

Ronaldo
The gifted and one-time most expensive player in history spent the 2002 World Cup sporting a bizarre triangle of hair on the front of his head. The star striker later claimed that he decided to sport the 'wedge' after his young son kept confusing him with team-mate Roberto Carlos while watching on television.

Jason Lee
The 90s striker was brought close to tears by the chant, 'He's got a pineapple on his head', which followed him from ground to ground. The chant, he claims, ruined his game.

Kevin Keegan
Who can forget the perm that might, just might, have been fashionable in the late 70s, but which Keegan insisted on keeping for most of the 80s while splashing on his Brut.

JUDAS
There is an old saying that you should never mess on your neighbour's doorstep. Never is it more apt than in football, and it particularly applies to the 'traitors' who dare switch from their club to the local rivals. Some, however, got away with it and remain loved on both sides of the garden fence. Supporters rarely seem to remember that footballers are employees and not supporters of the club

they play for and so we have the traditional, and not too original shout of: 'Judas!'

Alan Smith – Leeds United to Manchester United 2004
The hometown striker was mobbed by Leeds fans on the Elland Road pitch after the relegated club's final home game of the season. Just weeks later they were ready to string Smith up as he put his boyhood loyalties aside and joined the arch-enemy at Old Trafford.

Rio Ferdinand – Leeds United to Manchester United 2002
The cultured centre-back's impressive performances at the World Cup in the Far East in 2002 brought Alex Ferguson knocking, and a world record fee for a defender was more than the Elland Road club could resist. But selling their best player to their most bitter rivals meant the fans are still not happy.

Sol Campbell – Tottenham Hotspur to Arsenal, 2001
Not only did the club captain leave, he did so on a free transfer to Spurs' nearest neighbours, and most bitter enemies. To mention his name at White Hart Lane is still a dangerous pastime. Not that Sol seemed to be bothered the way he celebrated winning the title there in 2004.

Luis Figo – Barcelona to Real Madrid, 2000
The Portuguese winger felt the wrath of the whole of Catalonia when he left Barcelona for the aristocratic club of the King of Spain. Even a then world record fee failed to appease the Barca fans, who somehow managed to smuggle a pig's head into the Nou Camp to hurl at their former hero when he returned with Madrid in 2002.

Nick Barmby – Everton to Liverpool, 2000
The England midfielder crossed Stanley Park, saying he wanted to play for his boyhood-favourite Reds. The Toffee's fans were even more annoyed when he scored in the derby against his old team.

Luis Enrique – Real Madrid to Barcelona, 1996
Back when Barca were the more successful of the Spanish giants, they tempted the combative Spanish midfielder to quit the Bernabeu. It took a while for him to be accepted at the Nou Camp, but he eventually won the fans over and was given the captain's armband.

Eric Cantona – Leeds United to Manchester United, 1992
After inspiring Leeds to their first league title in 18 years, the French striker was controversially sold to their arch-rivals, amid claims of a dressing room bust-up. He went on to become a legend at Old Trafford, winning four Premier League titles.

Paul Ince – West Ham United to Manchester United, 1989
The Hammers and the Red Devils are hardly historical rivals, but Ince totally angered the Upton Park faithful by appearing in a Manchester United shirt before the transfer was complete. Continues to get a red-hot reception at the Boleyn, whoever he is fouling for.

Mo Johnston – Glasgow Celtic (via Nantes) to Glasgow Rangers 1989
The prolific Scottish striker, a Catholic, caused a massive outcry when he signed for Rangers. So much so, that some of the Rangers hardcore Protestant fans were seen burning season tickets and scarves when former Celtic favourite Johnston arrived.

A FEW EXCEPTIONS TO THE RULE

Pat Jennings – Tottenham Hotspur to Arsenal, 1977
When Spurs released their Northern Irish goalkeeper, they thought his skills were on the wane. He played for another seven years at Arsenal, playing in three successive FA Cup finals and a European

FANTASTIC FOOTBALL FACTS

Cup-Winners' Cup final too. He is still fondly remembered on both sides of the North London divide.

Denis Law – Manchester United to Manchester City, 1973
The hero of the Stretford End, Law was given a free transfer to the blue half of Manchester. He then helped relegate his beloved Reds with a back heel on the last day of the season. Despite this, he is still adored at Old Trafford.

IS THAT A RECORD? – FOOTBALL SONGS

Despite numerous attempts to combine the fields of football and music, there have been very few football songs that would have actually charted on their musical merits alone. After all these years football songs still fall into two distinct categories, the rubbish cup final records, and the rubbish World Cup records.

Abide With Me (1927); Chart Position: none
Words: Henry F. Lyte, 1793–1847
Music: William H. Monk, 1823–1889
The first ever 'football song', it was sung by the crowd at the Arsenal v Cardiff FA Cup final at Wembley Stadium, and remains a cup final crowd favourite to this day.

Back Home (1970); Chart Position: No. 1 in May
Words: William Wylie Martin
Music: Phil Coulter
England travelled to the World Cup in Mexico as holders and favourites. Arguably England's finest-ever team, they were, unfortunately, 'Back Home' earlier than hoped, losing their quarter-final, to Germany, in extra time.

Good Old Arsenal (1971); Chart Position: No. 16 in May
Words: Jimmy Hill
Music: 'Rule Britannia' composed by Thomas Augustine Arne
Arsenal's Cup final record, in their original double year, has the distinction of having been written by Jimmy Hill. Yes, THAT Jimmy Hill.

FANTASTIC FOOTBALL FACTS

Ossie's Dream (1981); Chart Position: No. 5 in May
Words: Chas Hodges and Dave Peacock
Music: Chas Hodges and Dave Peacock
Chas and Dave took the FA Cup song genre to a new level by releasing whole albums dedicated to their beloved club. Pick of the bunch has to be Tottenham's 1981 ditty 'Ossie's Dream', closely followed by 'Nice One Cyril' and 'When The Year Ends In A One.'

Anfield Rap (Red Machine In Full Effect) (1988); Chart Position: No. 3 in May
Words: Craig Johnston
Music: T Gray, H Gray & I Hoxley
Liverpool's unforgettable song accompanied a cup final defeat by lowly Wimbledon. The record is most memorable for John Barnes's rapping debut, years before his 'World in Motion skills', and Bruce Grobbelaar's huge comedy gloves.

World in Motion (1990); Chart Position: No. 1 in June
Words: Keith Allen and New Order
Music: New Order
The English effort for the World Cup was mostly performed by New Order, but it is the short rap by John Barnes that will live longest in the memory. Altogether now, 'You've got to hold and give...'

Nessun Dorma (1990); Chart Position: No. 2 in July
Words: Giacomo Puccini
Music: Giacomo Puccini
The official song for the World Cup in Italy. When hearing the Three Tenors belting out the football fans' favourite operatic aria, it is impossible not to recall Gazza's tears, and those horrible, horrible penalties.

Three Lions (1996); Chart Position: No. 1 June
Words: David Baddiel and Frank Skinner
Music: Ian Broudie
Baddiel and Skinner wrote the lyrics and were joined by The
Lightning Seeds on the most popular football song to date. Although
England failed to win the European Championships on home turf,
the song and the atmosphere it created will live on.

Vindaloo (1998); Chart Position: No. 2 in July
Words: Fat Les
Music: Fat Les
Fat Les is a group fronted by actor and comedian Keith Allen, Blur's
Alex James and controversial artist Damien Hirst among others.
Before the 1998 World Cup they cashed in on the football song mar-
ket generated by 'Three Lions' and its re-release. The lyrics told the
opposition 'We're gonna score one more than you!' True to football
song form, England failed to live up to the hype and lost to Argentina
in the second round.

TOP OF THE POPS
Just because they score a few goals, some footballers seem to think
they can take the music charts by storm. Boy, how wrong they can
be!

In honour of their efforts, here are the wingers-turned-singers
and weavers-turned-divas who are football's Top of the Pops.

Paul Gascoigne can claim the honour as the highest-ranking soccer
star in the charts. On the back of his popularity in the 1990 World
Cup Finals, he made it all the way to No. 2 following a collaboration
with Lindisfarne on the smash hit 'Fog on the Tyne'.

However, most people have long forgotten Gazza's follow-up
effort 'Geordie Boys' which just failed to emulate his initial success
– climbing all the way to No. 31.

FANTASTIC FOOTBALL FACTS

Bizarrely enough, Kevin Keegan – the man whose boots Gascoigne used to clean as an apprentice at Newcastle – had also reached No. 31 in the charts back in 1979 with 'Head Over Heels In Love'. This single was written by Chris Norman and Peter Spencer from the band Smokie, allegedly about leather queen Suzi Quatro.

Andy Cole, who played under Keegan at Newcastle, also tried his hand at music with a dance track entitled 'Outstanding'. However, despite a Supakings Sucker Punch Mix and The Champions Double Treble Mix, the 2000 single failed to trouble the Top 40.

Former England manager Terry Venables is another football star to be denied a chart entry. He unsuccessfully tried his luck with 'What Do You Want To Make Those Eyes At Me For' back in 1974 and did little better when he released a World Cup 2002 anthem called 'England Crazy'.

2002 was also the year that one-time commentator Ron Atkinson attempted to croon his way to a festive No. 1 with 'It's Christmas – Let's Give Love A Try'.
   Unfortunately, his letter to Santa must have gone missing as Girls Aloud claimed the honour with Ron nowhere in sight.

Christian Dailly is the most high-profile current footballer to get involved with music. The West Ham defender is lead singer and guitarist for a rock band called South Playground, who had previously been known, somewhat controversially, as Hooligan.

Glenn Hoddle and Chris Waddle are perhaps the most cringeworthy chart footballers following their memorable appearance on *Top of the Pops* back in 1987. Their rock ballad Diamond Lights eventually reached No. 12, although whether either of them has ever lived it down is debatable.

And it's not just in England that star footballers get tempted into releasing bizarre singles. Johan Cruyff reached No. 21 in the Dutch charts in 1969 with the fantastically named tune 'Oei, Oei, Oei'. And Pele was credited on the 1977 track 'Meu Mondo E Uma Bola' alongside Garrincha.

Meanwhile, former Spurs and Scotland striker Steve Archibald is believed to be the first singer ever to appear on *Top of the Pops* twice on the same night with different songs. Back in 1982 he lent his voice to the Tottenham FA Cup Final tune originally entitled 'Tottenham, Tottenham', having already featured on the Scotland World Cup single 'We Have a Dream'.

However, Spurs team-mates Ray Clemence and Glenn Hoddle quickly achieved the same feat as they then dashed across the studio to feature in the England World Cup anthem 'We'll Take More Care of You (Fly the Flag)'.

CAN YOU HEAR US ON THE BOX?

Football supporters are renowned for their witty humour and ability to humiliate opposing teams and fans.

Here we list some of the terrace chants which, although widely heard, still bring a chuckle to the most hardcore of fans.

Away in a manger,
No crib for a bed,
The little Lord Jesus looked up and he said:
'We hate Tottenham, and we hate Tottenham.'
(Arsenal fans to Tottenham supporters)

You won the league in black and white,
You won the league in black and white,
You won the league in the 60s,
You won the league in black and white
(Often used against Tottenham and Chelsea)

FANTASTIC FOOTBALL FACTS

Chim chiminee,
Chim chiminee,
Chim chim, cheroo
We hate those b*****s in claret and blue.
(Birmingham supporters to Aston Villa fans)

Stick the blue flag up yer arse,
Stick the blue flag up yer arse,
The black and white you'll never pass,
Stick yer blue flag up yer arse.
(Fulham fans turn Chelsea's famous chant against them)

Now if you go down Goodison Way
Hard luck stories you hear each day
There's not a trophy to be seen
Cos Liverpool have swept them clean
Now on the glorious 10th of May
There's laughing reds on Wembley Way
We're full of smiles and joy and glee
It's Everton 1 and Liverpool 3
Now on the 20th of May
We're laughing still on Wembley Way
Those Evertonians feeling blue
At Liverpool 3 and Everton 2
And as we sang round Goodison Park
With crying blues all in a nark
They're probably crying still
At Liverpool 5 and Everton nil.
(Liverpool fans remind their Everton counterparts of famous victories down the years)

One-nil down
Two-one up
Michael Owen won the cup
With a top-class Paddy pass, gave the lad the ball
Poor old Arsenal won sod all
(Liverpool supporters celebrate the 2001 FA Cup final win over Arsenal)

In your Sunderland slums,
In your Sunderland slums,
You look in the dustbin for something to eat,
You find a dead rat and you think it's a treat,
In your Sunderland slums
(Middlesbrough supporters use this popular chant against their local rivals)

Nayim from the halfway line,
Nayim from the halfway line,
(Tottenham fans recall David Seaman's howler for Arsenal in the 1995 Cup-Winners' cup final)

You're just a small town in Oldbury
You're just a small town in Oldbury
(Wolves fans to West Brom supporters)

Come in a taxi
You must have come in a taxi
Come in a taxi
You must have come in a taxi
(A chant used to make fun of a small travelling contingent)

FANTASTIC FOOTBALL FACTS

I gotta shed
It's bigger than this
I gotta shed that's bigger than this
It's got a door and a window
I got a shed that's bigger than this
My rabbit hutch
Is bigger than this
My rabbit hutch is bigger than this
It's got a door and a rabbit
My rabbit hutch is bigger than this
(Away fans question the facilities at the home ground)

What's it like to,
What's it like to,
What's it like to see a crowd
What's it like to see a crowd
(Travelling fans suggest the home attendances are not usually very high)

Back to the Conference
You're going back to the Conference
Back to the Conference,
You're going back to the Conference
(A popular chant in Division Three against the fans of newly-promoted sides)

All we want is a decent referee (clap clap)
A decent referee (clap clap)
A decent referee (clap clap)
All we want is a decent referee (clap clap)
(Fans unite against the common enemy, the referee, as they adopt the tune to 'The Yellow Submarine')

One song, you've only got one song
(Used against fans who obviously haven't read this page!)

GET YOUR KIT OFF

Many people can look in their wardrobe and find some shocking clothes that they believed at one time were the height of fashion. Football fans have more guilty secrets than most; here are some of the kits that the players and fans should like to forget.

Birmingham City

In the mid-70s they set the bench mark in fashion faux pas with their kit which combined a large yellow stripe in the middle with a brown panel and sleeve on one side and a gaudy navy blue on the other. Outstanding.

Coventry City

In 1978 the Sky Blues could be seen in a chocolate brown away kit, as memorable as the moustache of Terry Yorath and the bouffant of Ian Wallace who played in the strip.

Arsenal

Who could forget the visually offensive, though not unsuccessful, yellow away kit bespeckled with green triangles, as modelled by Anders Limpar and Ian Selley.

Everton

The salmon pink away strip of the early 90s was more fitting for London's 'Pride' festival than the cut and thrust of the football field. Maybe they were chasing the pink pound.

Juventus

They followed Everton's lead with their fey offering in 1997 which somehow undermined Antonio Conte's 'hardman' image.

FANTASTIC FOOTBALL FACTS

Derby County
The Rams' gaudy third-choice kit of the 80s was described by a local radio commentator of the time as 'their Moulin Rouge tarts' outfit.'

Bristol Rovers
Fans may choose to forget their rather fetching lemon and tangerine quartered kit of the 1987–88 season. Truly awful.

Southend United
In 1997 and again in 1998 Southend were relegated because of their results, but if there was any justice it should have been for their kit that appeared to have a large yellow bird dropping splattered on the front of their blue shirts.

Hull City
In 1992 Hull sported an appalling yet comical 'tiger stripes' kit, much to the derision of opposition fans. Grrrrrrrr.

Jorge Campos
The undisputed king of the awful shirt. Mexican keeper Campos became famous for his numerous George Melly-style fluorescent psychedelic shirts that would have been better served as a TV test card.

FASHION DISASTERS
Football and fashion have had an uneasy relationship down the years, as Barry Venison's suits on ITV have proved. Players may think that being trendy is easy given their massive wage packets, but sometimes they can get it horribly wrong. Having said that the managers can be just as bad and occasionally the clubs themselves need a warning from the Fashion Police.

Liverpool players, then known as the Spice Boys, stunned fans at the 1996 FA Cup final by emerging for the pre-match walkabout on the Wembley turf in white suits.

Goalkeeper David James took the blame due to his modelling contract with Armani and even team-mate Robbie Fowler admitted: 'When we turned up in those white suits, everyone thought we were the band.'

The day got even worse for the Merseysiders as they lost to arch-rivals Manchester United 1–0, thanks to Eric Cantona's goal, to allow Alex Ferguson's side to clinch the Double.

Robbie Fowler later spawned a mini-trend among thousands of Sunday League players when he began to wear a noseband.

The striker, then at Liverpool, claimed the thin plastic strip increased air intake and improved his performance.

However, a team of American scientists at the University of Buffalo carried out tests and spokesman Frank Cerny said: 'We wanted to see if the strips, when worn correctly, have any effect at this level of performance. The answer is they don't.'

David Beckham, seemingly always keen to start a new trend, however bizarre, sent the newspapers into a frenzy in June 1998 when he was photographed wearing a sarong in Nice, in the south of France.

The Jean-Paul Gaultier item apparently cost £150 and caused a sensation as tabloids used up hundreds of column inches debating whether men could or should be seen in public in a skirt.

Beckham himself revealed in his autobiography, *My Side*: 'I bought the infamous sarong when I was out with Mel B's ex-husband, Jimmy, in Paris. In fact, I liked it so much, I bought several in different colours.'

While all the top stars try to make their fashion statements off the pitch with the latest styles from Gucci, Prada and Armani, it takes a special kind of player to become the king of cool on the field.

FANTASTIC FOOTBALL FACTS

Faroe Islands goalkeeper Jens Knudsen took on the challenge in the mid-1990s as he attempted to make the bobble hat the top accessory for stylish shot-stoppers. Unbelievably, the trend never took off.

Another hat had been prominent in 1976 as Malcolm Allison attempted to make history by guiding a Third Division side, Crystal Palace, to the FA Cup final.

Rival fans were more than keen to deride Allison's lucky fedora hat which he claimed had helped Palace reach the semi-finals.

In the end, though, the Palace boss was forced to take his hat off to Southampton who beat his side and then went on to claim an unlikely victory over Manchester United at Wembley to lift the trophy.

David Pleat maintained the penchant for managerial fashion faux-pas while celebrating Luton Town's survival in Division 1 in 1983. The Hatters had just beaten Man City 1–0 at Maine Road to stay up, but most people only remember Pleat dancing onto the pitch in a mind-blowing brown suit and cream loafers.

Raddy Antic, who scored the Luton goal, recalls: 'The memory of David jumping across the pitch will live with me all my life.'

In more recent years, Edgar Davids has appeared keen to introduce a certain chic onto the pitch, although he at least had a medical excuse.

The Dutchman was diagnosed with glaucoma in 1999 and, thanks to special permission from FIFA, has worn protective goggles during matches ever since. Davids might think he looks cool, but team-mate Jaap Stam is rumoured to have once joked in the dressing room before a match: 'Come on Edgar, we're playing football, you haven't got time to go skiing.'

Football clubs are wise nowadays to marketing gimmicks, but back in the 1970s it came as something of a shock when Leeds

United players ran out with nifty little sock tags showing their number.

The idea was the brainwave of Roy of the Rovers comic artist Paul Trevillion, but failed to gain widespread appeal.

Kit modifications can get teams into trouble, though. In 2003 Cameroon opted to wear an all-in-one strip, incorporating a fetching lions maul rip-effect, at the African Nations Cup. FIFA were not impressed and, insisting that their rules only permitted the use of separate shorts and shirts, fined the Cameroon FA £86,000 and deducted six points from their 2006 World Cup qualifying campaign, although they were later handed back.

BIZARRE INJURIES

Groin strains and pulled hamstrings are part and parcel of foot-ballers' lives. But occasionally they fall foul of rather more bizarre injuries.

Cheltenham's Damian Spencer injured his knee and split open a hand when tripping over a plastic dog bone and falling down the stairs.

Portsmouth's John Durnin crashed his golf buggy into a fairway hollow and sustained a dislocated elbow.

Wolves striker Robbie Keane damaged his ankle when he trod on his TV remote controller.

Liverpool's Mark Kennedy was ruled out after damaging tendons in his hand pulling on a training-ground bib.

Chelsea defender Celestine Babayaro sustained a broken ankle while executing a celebratory somersault during a pre-season match.

Alan Wright of Aston Villa had to ditch his £50,000 Ferrari after he developed a knee problem because of the position of the accelerator. The defender opted for a Rover 400 instead.

Tottenham's Allan Nielsen was sidelined when his new-born daughter poked him in the eye.

Liverpool goalkeeper Michael Stensgaard was forced into temporary retirement after he injured his shoulder trying to stop an ironing board from falling over.

FANTASTIC FOOTBALL FACTS

Arsenal match-winner Steve Morrow suffered a broken arm when team-mate Tony Adams hoisted him in the air then dropped him after the 1993 League Cup final against Sheffield Wednesday.

Chelsea goalkeeper Dave Beasant missed the start of the season after dropping a jar of salad cream on his foot.

Spain goalkeeper Santiago Canizares was forced to miss the 2002 World Cup after he dropped a bottle of cologne on his foot and severed a tendon.

Chelsea's John Terry wrenched his ankle while watching a Wimbledon semi-final between Tim Henman and Lleyton Hewitt.

THE WORST EXCUSES
No one likes losing in football – but some managers and players have gone to extreme lengths to explain an embarrassing defeat.
   Here we list some of the lame excuses used by those in the football world.

Liverpool 0 Arsenal 2, 26 May 1989
Arsenal travelled to Anfield having to win by two clear goals to win the league title. In the final minute, Michael Thomas scored one of the most famous league goals to win the championship for the Gunners, but Liverpool defender Alan Hansen did not believe the result was down to skill. No, Hansen blamed the fact that the game was played on a Friday night and insisted Liverpool would have won the title if it had been played on a Saturday!

Arsenal 2 Liverpool 1, 8 May 1971
Emlyn Hughes blamed an FA Cup final defeat by Arsenal on the new kit Liverpool were wearing. Hughes and his team-mates claimed the wool shirts were 'too heavy'.

Newcastle 5 Manchester United 0, 20 October 1996

After Newcastle thrashed Manchester United in 1996, Alex Ferguson blamed his side's defeat on tiredness caused by a plane journey after playing against Fenerbahce in Turkey.

Southampton 6 Manchester United 3, 26 October 1996

Alex Ferguson blamed Manchester United's embarrassing defeat at Southampton on the fact his players could not see one another!

Ferguson suggested his team's new grey strip left his players unable to pick out their team-mates as they blended in with the background!

Stevenage 1 Newcastle 1, 25 January 1998

After Premiership Newcastle United could only draw at Conference side Stevenage in the FA Cup, furious manager Kenny Dalglish moaned that the balls were 'too bouncy'!

Holland – Euro 2000

As Holland struggled to make an impact on Euro 2000, manager Frank Rijkaard put his team's misfortune down to a love of cards, saying that too much time dealing around the table had distracted them.

Lee Chapman – Leeds

Chapman once blamed the pitch after missing a sitter for Leeds at Elland Road. He claimed that rugby side Hunslet had churned up the pitch – but they had not even started playing on the ground at that stage!

Chris Mooney – Rotherham

Rotherham goalkeeper Chris Mooney once let a tame effort straight through his legs. However, rather than accept the mistake as his, Mooney insisted it was due to blinded vision caused by the shine from his centre-half's bald head.

FANTASTIC FOOTBALL FACTS

Gerard Houllier – Liverpool

The Frenchman could fill this section on his own for his increasingly bizarre comments as he steered Liverpool further and further away from the Premiership title.

Here are just a selection of the excuses he used to explain away a series of poor results ...

'Too many players were trying to score or create a goal.'

'It was not a mistake, it was a blunder.'

'You can't say my team aren't winners. They've proved that by finishing fourth, third and second in the last three years.'

'I read that people want to go back to the 60s and 70s culture. Well fair enough, but not with me.' A week later Houllier's reign was over!

RUDE BOYS

Sniggering at players' and bosses' unfortunate names may be considered puerile – but who cares. Fans up and down the country long for the day when they can hear John Motson screaming: 'And Ufarte passes to Pinas, who is sure to stand up against Bogie's tackle to shoot past Seaman for a goal!'

The definitive list of unfortunately named players is as follows:

Ian Bogie

The former Newcastle and Orient midfielder was once known as the 'new Gazza' – possibly because he was notorious for getting up players' noses.

Alan Dicks

Former Fulham manager, whose poor results led to fans holding up banners with the unfortunate slogan 'Dicks Out'. Thankfully, only Alan obliged.

Gilles Fuchs
The French former Lyon player, who was the subject of the classic headline 'Fuchs off to Benfica'.

Kanu
Not very funny, until you remember the Arsenal and Nigeria striker's first name is Nwankwo.

Georg Koch
The six-foot five-inch goalkeeper was recently linked with Southampton, which led to the tabloid story that began: 'Saints are looking to get their hands on a big German Koch!'

Stefan Kuntz
After the German had equalised against England in Euro 96 – and the home side then went out on penalties – distraught fans couldn't help screaming the midfielder's surname. He is now a manager at LR Ahlen.

Brian Pinas
Dutch midfielder who caused great titters on Tyneside when he signed for Newcastle United in 1997. Sadly he only kept it up for one season before being sold to Feyenoord.

David Seaman
For some reason the ex-England goalkeeper's nickname at Arsenal was H (cockney rhyming slang) or Spunky.

Danny Shittu
The QPR defender's name was made even more funny when he was joined on the team sheet by Doudou.

Lopez Ufarte
Former Real Sociedad and Spain forward who featured in his team's 1982 World Cup campaign. Ran like the wind apparently.

FANTASTIC FOOTBALL FACTS

MEMORABLE CELEBRATIONS

Goal celebrations have evolved from a polite shake of the hand followed by a 'well done old bean' to 'boy band' levels of dance choreography. Here are some of the most memorable ones that we have enjoyed over recent years from the more colourful characters in our game.

Lomana LuaLua

His trademark somersaulting goal celebrations have been enjoyed by the fans of Colchester, Newcastle and now Portsmouth. The striker performs a spectacular gymnastic display which sees him turning head over heels in mid-air.

Julius Agahowa

He performed a breathtaking SEVEN successive somersaults after he scored for Nigeria in their 2–1 defeat to Sweden in the 2002 World Cup.

Paul Gascoigne

Created the now legendary 'Dentist Chair' celebrations after he scored a superb goal against Scotland during Euro '96. This involved his England colleagues, Teddy Sheringham in particular, squirting drinks into a prostrate Gascoigne's mouth – a cheeky reference to revelations of excessive drinking while on a pre-tournament tour in the Far East.

Robbie Fowler

'The class "A" celebration'. After scoring for Liverpool, against fierce rivals Everton, Fowler got down on all fours in front of the away fans and pretended to snort the touchline. Blues fans who had constantly accused him of taking cocaine were not amused, while Reds manager Gerard Houllier bizarrely claimed his striker was actually pretending to be a grazing cow.

Lee Sharpe

In his playing days with Manchester United the flying winger used to impersonate Elvis after scoring. His dance, nicknamed 'The Sharpey Shuffle,' involved him twirling hips (à la Elvis circa 1956) at the corner flags to the delight of the fans.

Gordon Strachan

The ginger ninja scored for Manchester United against the all conquering Liverpoool team of the day and to celebrate he took a huge puff on an imaginary cigar.

Sol Campbell

The giant centre-back scored a towering header against Argentina and wheeled away in absolute ecstasy to be mobbed by his team-mates – only to find out that the goal was disallowed.

Roberto Di Matteo

He summed up Ruud Gullit's 'sexy football' after he scored on his debut against Middlesbrough at the start of the 1996–97 season and he lay on his side with one finger aloft before being joined by a number of his Chelsea team-mates.

Temuri Ketsbaia

The Georgian kicked seven bells out of the advertising hoardings in a berserk rage after he scored at St James's Park. Goodness knows what he would do if he was upset!

Stuart Pearce

For sheer passion the most memorable image is that of Stuart Pearce waving his clenched fist and shouting 'Come On' to the crowd after slotting home his penalty against Spain in the nail-biting shoot-out at Euro '96.

FANTASTIC FOOTBALL FACTS

Ian Wright and Neil Ruddock
The two re-created Paolo di Canio's famous pushing of referee Paul Alcock – who fell to floor 'like a girl'.

Roger Milla
In Italia '90 the Cameroonian 'dirty danced' with the corner flag to celebrate.

CLUB NICKNAMES
Most clubs' nicknames come from either the site of their ground or the colour of their strip – hence the myriad of 'Reds' and 'Blues' throughout the leagues – but others are a little more cryptic.

Arsenal – Gunners
The Highbury club have been known as the Gunners since the days when they were a factory team for the Royal Arsenal at Woolwich where army hardware was made.

West Bromwich Albion – Baggies
Strangely enough, the reason behind West Brom's name is due to the fact the shorts they used to wear were on the large side.

Charlton Athletic – Addicks
Charlton got their fishy nickname from a story relating how a local fishmonger, Arthur Bryan, used to provide the team with post-match haddocks in the early days of the club.

Everton – Toffees
Two stories battle for the honour of Everton's nickname. There was a shop known as Mother Nobblett's Toffee shop near Goodison Park, where the club moved from Anfield in 1894. But near the Queen's Head Hotel, where Everton first held their meetings, stood Ye Ancient Everton Toffee House.

Bolton Wanderers – Trotters
A Trotter is an old Lancashire word for practical joker, and the club that formed as an offshoot from the Christ Church Sunday School side were apparently renowned for japes. The reason why they broke away from the church side was that the vicar laid down too many rules. Like no practical jokes, maybe?

Norwich City – Canaries
It may seem obvious that a yellow-clad team would be called the Canaries. But the name is made even more fitting when you learn that between 1908 and 1935 they played at The Nest.

Southampton – Saints
When the club first formed in 1885, they were known as Southampton St Mary's, after the church of the same name. Two years later they dropped the religious part of their name, but the nickname stuck. And in 2001, when they moved from The Dell, it was revived as part of the stadium name.

Sunderland – Black Cats
When Sunderland moved from Roker Park to the Stadium of Light in 1997, their former nicknames of the Rokerites and the Rokermen became irrelevant. So the club's website asked fans to choose between the Black Cats, the Light Brigade, the Miners, the Sols and the Mackems, with over half of the 11,000 voters choosing their current nickname.

GOALS GALORE

Goals are the lifeblood of football. Here are some of the record-breaking achievements at international and domestic level.

MOST IN A GAME

13 – Archie Thompson in Australia's 31–0 rout of American Samoa in a World Cup qualifier at Coff's Harbour, New South Wales, in April 2001.

13 – John Petrie in Arbroath's 36–0 scoreline against Bon Accord in a Scottish Cup first-round tie in September 1885.

10 – Joe Payne for Luton, who put 12 past Bristol Rovers without reply in a Division 3 South match in April 1936.

9 – Ted MacDougall for Bournemouth in their 11–0 FA Cup first round defeat of Margate in November 1971.

6 – Frank Bunn in Oldham's 7–0 victory over Scarborough in a League Cup third round tie in October 1989.

5 – Andy Cole for Manchester United in a 9–0 win over Ipswich in March 1995. Cole shares the record for the best individual tally in the Premiership with Alan Shearer, who netted five for Newcastle in their 8–0 win over Sheffield Wednesday in September 1999.

5 – Kenny Miller for Rangers who beat St Mirren 7–1 in November 2000 and Paul Sturrock for Dundee United in their 7–0 defeat of Morton in November 1984 – both Scottish Premier matches.

FANTASTIC FOOTBALL FACTS

MOST IN A SEASON

66 in 38 games – Jimmy Smith for Ayr United in the 1927–28 Scottish Division 2 season.

60 in 39 games – Dixie Dean for Everton in the 1927–28 Division 1 season.

35 in 35 games – Brian McClair for Celtic in the 1986–87 Scottish Premier Division

35 in 37 games – Henrik Larsson for Celtic in the 2000–01 Scottish Premier Division.

34 in 40 games – Andy Cole for Newcastle in the 1993–94 Premiership.

34 in 42 games – Alan Shearer for Blackburn in the 1994–95 Premiership.

20 in 8 games – Jimmy Ross in the FA Cup for Preston during their 1887–88 campaign.

12 in 9 games – Clive Allen in the League Cup for Tottenham during their 1986–87 campaign.

MOST IN CAREER

1,282 – The total reputedly scored by Pele for his club Santos and Brazil (1956–77), although many came in friendly matches for Santos.

434 – Arthur Rowley's tally in the Football League (1947–65) for West Brom, Fulham, Leicester, Shrewsbury.

410 – Jimmy McGrory's Scottish League total for Celtic and Clydebank (1922–38).

349 – The most scored for one Football League club by Dixie Dean for Everton (1925–37).

49 – Bobby Charlton's record international total for England (1958–70).

44 – Ian Rush's FA Cup goals for Liverpool, Newcastle and Chester (1979–98).

SCORING SEQUENCES

Steve Bloomer scored 19 goals in 10 successive appearances for England (1895–99).

Tom Phillipson netted in 13 successive Division 2 matches for Wolves in season 1926–27.

Ruud van Nistelrooy set a new Premiership record by scoring in nine consecutive Manchester United appearances, 14 goals in total. The run included the last eight matches of the 2002–03 season and the first game of the 2003–04 season.

Jimmy Greaves was the Division 1 leading marksman six times in 11 seasons (1958–69), twice for Chelsea and four times for Tottenham.

Denis Law scored all six goals for Manchester City in an FA Cup fourth round tie at Luton in January 1961 – and none of them counted. The match was abandoned after 69 minutes because of a waterlogged pitch when the score was 6–2. Law also scored his side's goal when the match was replayed, but they were beaten 3–1.

Geoff Hurst totalled 21 cup goals in the 1965–66 season – eleven in the League Cup, four in the FA Cup, and two in the Cup-Winners' Cup for West Ham, and four for England in the World Cup, three of them in the 4–2 win over West Germany in the final.

FANTASTIC FOOTBALL FACTS

Dixie McNeill netted in 10 successive FA Cup ties for Wrexham, a total of 18 goals, spread across three seasons (1977–80).

Alan Cork scored in all four divisions of the Football League, and in the Premiership, during his career with Wimbledon, Sheffield United and Fulham 1977–95.

When Oxford beat Shrewsbury 6–0 in Division 2 in April 1996, all the goals were headers – from Paul Moody (2), Stuart Massey, David Rush, Joey Beauchamp and Matt Murphy.

Ruud van Nistelrooy was on the mark in eight successive Premiership games for Manchester United in both the 2001–02 and 2002–03 campaigns.

SHARPSHOOTERS

Sometimes it pays to chance your arm – or rather your foot – straight from the kick off. Hoofing the ball goalwards, particularly if the wind is at your back, or launching a surprise attack can work wonders, as these goals show.

2.8 secs – Marc Burrows, Cowes Sports FC v Eastleigh Reserves, April 2004

2.8 secs – Ricardo Olivera, Rio Negro v Soriano, Uruguayan League, December 1998

4 secs – Jim Fryatt, Bradford PA v Tranmere, Division 4, April 1965

4 secs – Damian Mori, Adelaide v Sydney, Australian League, December 1995

5 secs – Malcolm Macdonald, Newcastle at St Johnstone, pre-season friendly, July 1972

6 secs – Albert Mundy, Aldershot v Hartlepool, Division 4, October 1958

6 secs – Barrie Jones, Notts County v Torquay, Division 3, March 1962

6 secs – Keith Smith, Crystal Palace v Derby, Division 2, December 1964

7 secs – Bobby Langton, Preston v Manchester City, Division 1, August 1948

8 secs – Davide Gualtieri, San Marino v England, World Cup qualifier (Bologna), November 1993

9 secs – John Hewitt, Aberdeen at Motherwell, Scottish Cup round 3, January 1982

PREMIERSHIP

10 secs – Ledley King, Tottenham at Bradford City, December, 2000

10 secs – Alan Shearer, Newcastle v Manchester City, January 2003

11 secs – Mark Viduka, Leeds v Charlton, March 2001

13 secs – Chris Sutton, Blackburn at Everton, April 1995

13 secs – Dwight Yorke, Aston Villa at Coventry, September 1995

HAT-TRICKS

Football nicked the term hat-trick from boring old cricket – a bowler who got three wickets in successive balls would be rewarded with a prize hat. Thierry Henry is more likely to trouser a few grand bonus when he nets three goals in a game these days. Here are some of the men who hit hat-tricks or better.

Scotland shocked England in their own backyard in 1928 when their 'Wembley Wizards' destroyed the home side and helped secure an amazing 5–1 win. Alex Jackson, who was the tallest Scottish striker

FANTASTIC FOOTBALL FACTS

despite standing just five foot seven, was the star as he grabbed a hat-trick, while Alex James added the other two.

England's supremacy over foreign opposition at Wembley came to an end when Hungary shocked them with a 6–3 win in a November 1953 friendly international, Nandor Hidegkuti scoring three times for the side who became known as the Magical Magyars.

Portugal were facing a shock defeat by North Korea when trailing 3–0 in a World Cup quarter-final at Goodison Park in July 1966, until Eusebio came to their rescue with four goals in a 5–3 victory.

Geoff Hurst became the first – and so far the only – player to score three goals in a World Cup final, when England defeated West Germany 4–2 after extra time at Wembley in July 1966.

No England player had scored five goals in one match until Malcolm Macdonald, single-handedly, gave them a 5–0 win over Cyprus in a European Championship qualifier at Wembley in May 1975.

Gary Lineker's scoring instincts were never sharper than the day he netted all three goals in a 3–0 win over Poland in the World Cup Finals in Monterrey, Mexico, in June 1986.

Alan Shearer, at 17, became the youngest player to score a Division 1 hat-trick on his full debut for Southampton in their 4–2 win over Arsenal in April 1988.

Dutch master Marco van Basten scored all three goals as Holland beat England 3–1 in Dusseldorf in June 1988 on their way to the European Championship.

Michael Owen's treble in a remarkable 5–1 win over Germany in Munich in September 2001 put England back on track for the World Cup Finals after they had lost to the same side at Wembley.

Robert Pires and Jermaine Pennant each scored three times in Arsenal's

6-1 home win over Southampton in May 2003 – the Premiership's first hat-trick double.

Thierry Henry became the first Arsenal player to score back-to-back hat-tricks at Highbury for more than half a century with three goals in a 4–2 win over Liverpool and four in the 5–0 victory over Leeds in April 2004.

HAT-TRICK SPECIALISTS

Dixie Dean, who played for Tranmere, Everton, Notts County and England, holds the record for the most career hat-tricks – 37 between 1924 and 1938.

George Camsell scored the most hat-tricks in one season – nine – for Middlesbrough in the 1926–27 Division 2 campaign.

Since the war, the most recorded in the top division was six by Chelsea's Jimmy Greaves in season 1960–61.

Alan Shearer holds the Premiership record of five, for Blackburn in the 1995–96 season.

In November 1987, Tony Adcock, Paul Stewart and David White all scored hat-tricks for Manchester City in a 10–1 win over Huddersfield in Division 2.

When West Ham beat Newcastle 8–1 in a Division 1 match in April 1986, Alvin Martin scored three times against three different goal-keepers – Martin Thomas injuring a shoulder and being replaced, in turn, by outfield players Chris Hedworth and Peter Beardsley.

MIRACLE MATCHES

Just how far in front does a team have to be to start celebrating? Spectators at these remarkable matches must have thought they could hear the Fat Lady singing long before the final whistle.

FANTASTIC FOOTBALL FACTS

Sheffield Wednesday 5 **Everton** 5
Wednesday earned a Division 1 point in November 1904 after trailing 5–0 at half-time.

Northampton 6 **Luton** 5
Northampton retrieved a 5–1 interval deficit to win this Division 3 South game on Boxing Day 1927.

Charlton 7 **Huddersfield** 6
Losing 5–1 with 28 minutes left of a Division 2 match in December 1957, and reduced to ten men by injury, Charlton staged a remarkable recovery, with left-winger Johnny Summers scoring five times.

Werder Bremen 5 **Anderlecht** 3
A major transformation in this Champions League group match in December 1993, saw Bremen scoring five times in 23 minutes in the second half after going in 3–0 behind.

Barnsley 3 **Ipswich** 3
Ian Marshall scored two of Ipswich's three goals which all came in the last five minutes of this Division 1 game in March 1996.

Port Vale 4 **Queen's Park Rangers** 4
Rangers' fighting spirit earned them a point in a Division 1 fixture in January 1997, John Spencer's goal bringing the sides level after Port Vale had led 4–1 with five minutes remaining.

Leeds 4 **Derby** 3
Lee Bowyer's 90th-minute winner crowned Leeds' Premiership comeback after their opponents were three goals to the good after 33 minutes in November 1997.

Tranmere 4 **Southampton** 3
Trailing 3–0 at half-time, Tranmere roared back in this FA Cup replay in February 2001 to reach the quarter-finals. Paul Rideout scored a hat-trick, then laid on the winner for substitute Stuart Barlow.

Deportivo La Coruna 4 **Paris St-Germain** 3
A hat-trick by Walter Pandiani sparked the Spanish team's comeback after they trailed 3–0 following 55 minutes of a Champions League second group fixture in March 2001.

Tottenham 3 **Manchester United** 5
David Beckham was among the scorers as United, 3–0 down at the break, turned this Premiership match on its head in September 2001.

Basle 3 **Liverpool** 3
One of Liverpool's best European comebacks after they went 3–0 down in 29 minutes. But it was still not enough to prevent them from Champions League group elimination in November 2002.

Tottenham 3 **Manchester City** 4
Kevin Keegan's City side looked down and out as Tottenham took a 3–0 half-time lead in an FA Cup fourth-round replay in February 2004. City also had Joey Barton sent off, but produced a memorable comeback capped by Jon Macken's headed winner.

RIGHT HAMMERINGS

From the first round of the Scottish Cup to World Cup qualifiers on the other side of the world, teams have shown no mercy to out-classed opponents. Here are the biggest spankings ever handed out in the history of football.

36–0 – Arbroath v Bon Accord, Scottish Cup 1st round, September 1885

35–0 – Dundee Harp v Aberdeen Rovers, Scottish Cup 1st round, September 1885

31–0 – Australia v American Samoa, World Cup qualifier, April 2001

26–0 – Preston v Hyde, FA Cup 1st round, October 1887

22–0 – Australia v Tonga, World Cup qualifier, April 2001

20–0 – Stirling Albion v Selkirk, Scottish Cup 1st round, December 1984

20–0 – Arbroath v Orion, Scottish Cup 1st round, September 1887

19–0 – Iran v Gaum, World Cup qualifier, November 2000

17–0 – Iran v Maldives, World Cup qualifier, June 1997

BIGGEST WINS IN THE WORLD CUP FINALS

10–1 – Hungary v El Salvador, Spain, June 1982

FANTASTIC FOOTBALL FACTS

9–0 – Hungary v South Korea, Switzerland, June 1954

9–0 – Yugoslavia v Zaire, West Germany, June 1974

RECORD VICTORIES IN THE PREMIERSHIP

9–0 – Manchester United v Ipswich, March 1995

8–0 – Newcastle v Sheffield Wednesday, September 1999

8–1 – Manchester United at Nottingham Forest, February 1999

7–0 – Manchester United v Barnsley, October 1997

7–0 – Blackburn v Nottingham Forest, November 1995

THEY'VE GOT THE RUNS

The successful teams and players are generally qualified by the number of medals they have won. But what about the achievements they make, that don't necessarily win them any silverware...

Arsenal – Longest scoring streak

The North London club broke the record by scoring in 55 successive Premiership fixtures. They scored in the last match of the season 2000–01, then in every match of their Championship winning-2001–02 season, and also in the first 16 of the 2002–03 season.

Chris Woods – Longest Shutout, British Football

While playing north of the Border for Glasgow Rangers England's keeper went 1,196 minutes without conceding a goal during the 1986–87 season.

Steve Death – Longest Shutout, English Football

Reading's keeper was unbeaten for 1,103 minutes in Division 4 in the 1978–79 season, which is an English league record.

Abel Resino – Longest Shutout, World Football
The Atletico Madrid keeper holds the World record, as he remained unbeaten for 1,275 minutes in the 1990–91 season.

Dino Zoff – Longest Shutout, International Football
The record in international football, belongs to Zoff and Italy, who didn't concede a goal for 1,142 minutes, between September 1972 and June 1974.

Arsenal – Longest Winning Streak
In the 2001–02 season the Gunners set a new English league record, by winning their last 13 matches – the most in one season. They then won their first game of the 2002–03 season and extended the record run to 14.

Nottingham Forest – Longest unbeaten League run
Brian Clough's side hold the English league record of 42 league matches unbeaten, notching up 21 wins and 21 draws, between November 1977 and December 1978.

Arsenal – League Season Unbeaten
In 2003–04 Arsenal became the first side to go through a top-flight league season unbeaten since Preston North End in 1888–89. The title-winning side from Highbury won 26 and drew 12 of their 38 matches home and away. Liverpool are the only other English team to have gone through a league season unbeaten, when they were Division 2 Champions in 1893–94.

Brazil – Longest Unbeaten Sequence, International Football
The South Americans hold the record for the longest unbeaten sequence in international football. They went 45 matches without defeat from 1993 to 1997.

FANTASTIC FOOTBALL FACTS

ORIGIN OF CLUB NAMES

Most names of football clubs are self-explanatory, as they are named after either the city or suburb in which they are based. But throughout the leagues there are a few puzzling anomalies ...

Arsenal

Workers at the Woolwich Royal Arsenal formed a football team in 1886, and first called their side Dial Square, after one of the work-shops at the southeast London factory. After former Nottingham Forest player Fred Beardsley asked his old club to supply shirts the side were known as the Woolwich Reds, but changed their name to Royal Arsenal by 1891.

Aston Villa

Formed when the Villa Cross Wesleyan Chapel Cricket team decided to play football in 1874. Games were hard to come by in Birmingham back then, and matches were often played half-rugby, half-football.

Scottish football enthusiast George Ramsay took over in 1876, and he is credited with beginning Villa's rise to the force they are today.

Crystal Palace

Palace was originally formed in 1861 by men in charge of the build-ing of the same name. It was forced to restructure after the FA did not like the idea of the company in charge of the then FA Cup final venue having a football team. They moved from the Cup final ground to Selhurst Park in 1915.

Leyton Orient

The Leyton bit of the Third Division strugglers' name is easy to work out. But Orient? It comes from an idea from a worker for the Orient Shipping Line in East London. The club changed their name from

Glyn to Clapton Orient in a bid to snare affluent fans from the area, but became Leyton Orient after they moved to their present home in E10.

Sheffield Wednesday

Like all great ideas, Sheffield Wednesday began in a pub. Members of Wednesday Cricket club – so-called because the team was largely made up of craftsmen who took Wednesday afternoon off – decided to start a football team in the Adelphi pub in Sheffield in 1867. On the site of the pub stands the Crucible Theatre, venue of the world snooker championships.

Port Vale

If you have ever travelled up the M1 and asked directions to Port Vale, you will know it doesn't exist. The Stoke-on-Trent club got their name from the venue of their inaugural meeting in 1876 – Port Vale house. They briefly changed their name to Burslem Port Vale after moving to that suburb, but dropped it in 1909.

Tottenham Hotspur

Harry Hotspur was a swashbuckling hero and was immortalised in Shakespeare's Henry IV. And back in 1882, there was a small group of kids in north London who thought Hotspur would be a great name for their new football club. The Tottenham was added soon after to avoid confusion with another club of the time called London Hotspur.

HOT SHOTS

A free kick on the edge of the box provides the perfect opportunity for a player to put the hours of practice on the training ground into effect. Here are some of the most memorable free kicks in the history of the game.

FANTASTIC FOOTBALL FACTS

David Beckham (England v Colombia) – Not only is David Beckham the world's best crosser of the ball, but he's also a prolific free-kick taker whose first England goal was a tremendous swerving strike which stranded Colombia's goalkeeper, and secured England's 2–0 victory in the 1998 World Cup Finals.

Paul Gascoigne (Tottenham Hotspur v Arsenal) – The 1991 Spurs v Arsenal FA Cup semi-final featured Gazza gracing the stage with a stunning, curling, dipping free kick which found the top corner of David Seaman's net from 35 yards. Yet Seaman still got the blame. Tottenham went on to record a 3–1 victory and, later, to win the final against Nottingham Forest.

Ronald Koeman (Holland v England) – England fans are not keen to remember the Dutch dead-ball master after he flipped a dipping free kick into the top corner which helped ensure a 2–0 win in Rotterdam and kept Graham Taylor's side out of the 1994 World Cup Finals.

Roberto Carlos (Brazil v France) – Widely touted as the greatest free kick of all time, Carlos took a fast bowler's run-up and powered a 40-yard swerving strike past the helpless Fabien Barthez as the hosts France, drew 1–1 with Brazil during Le Tournoi in 1997.

Gary McAllister (Liverpool v Everton) – Against local rivals Everton, this curling 44-yard dead-ball kick evaded the keeper's out-stretched fingertips and sneaked inside the right-hand post to clinch a 3–2 victory in the 2001 Merseyside derby.

Willie Carr (Coventry v Everton) – Carr and Ernie Hunt became famous for the 'donkey-kick' set-up – perhaps the most infamous free kick of all time, now banned. Carr held the ball at a free kick between his ankles and flicked the ball up for Hunt to volley home. The goal was allowed, but the FA ruled against its use again as it was deemed to be touching the ball twice. It was named in honour of Jeff Blockley – Coventry's immobile centre-half.

Sinisa Mihajlovic (Lazio v Chelsea) – Chelsea supporters will be keen to forget the Yugoslavian defender's stunning dead-ball winner for Lazio in the 1999–2000 Champions League, which found the top corner of goalkeeper Ed de Goey's net despite coming from an acute angle. Lazio ran out 2–1 winners.

Roberto Rivelino (Brazil v Czech) – Brazil's 70s star Rivelino was famous for his fabulous banana kicks – he virtually invented the art form. He made his name in the 1970 World Cup when Brazil beat Czechoslovakia 4–1. Rivelino completely wrong-footed the goal-keeper with his trademark kick, bending the ball around the wall and safely into the bottom right corner of the net.

Matt Le Tissier (Southampton v Wimbledon) – Often a source of memorable and sometimes unconventional free kicks during his career, perhaps most famously the only goal in a 1–0 over Wimbledon, when team-mate Jim Magilton provided a layback which Le Tiss casually chipped up and volleyed smartly into the top right-hand corner.

David Beckham (England v Greece) – Included if only for the time-liness of Beckham's final-minute intervention against Greece, during a crucial World Cup qualifier in 2001. England seemed doomed to another failed qualifying campaign and were trailing 2–1 until Becks' 30-yard free kick propelled them to the 2002 Finals.

ON THE SPOT

It's only 12 yards away from goal with just the keeper to beat, but the pressure involved means that scoring from a penalty can never be guaranteed. However, some players down the years were virtually unstoppable from the spot and whether 'placers' or 'blasters', we bring you the penalty kings.

FANTASTIC FOOTBALL FACTS

Matt Le Tissier is probably the most prolific penalty-taker of modern times. During his time at Southampton he netted 48 out of the 49 spot kicks he took.

His only miss came in a Premiership match against Nottingham Forest on 24 March 1993 when Mark Crossley saved his shot.

The only other man who can claim to have saved a Le Tissier penalty is Saints fan Steve Bull who achieved the remarkable feat as part of the pre-match entertainment before Southampton's first game of the 2002–03 season against Middlesbrough. Ironically enough, Crossley was sitting on the Boro bench that day!

Ray Stewart took responsibility 86 times when West Ham were awarded penalties during his 12–year Upton Park career between 1979 and 1991.

Of those, he only missed ten, although he personally claims that he managed to net another five goals from follow-ups!

Julian Dicks inherited the penalty mantle at West Ham following Ray Stewart's departure and enjoyed success from the spot thanks to his no-nonsense power technique.

However, his greatest milestone came following his transfer to Liverpool as he became the last player to score in front of the old Kop at Anfield when he converted a penalty against Ipswich in April 1994.

Eric Cantona quickly became a hero for Manchester United fans and not least because whenever there was a foul in the box the Frenchman would almost always deliver the ultimate punishment.

Cantona netted 17 out of his 19 penalties for United, including two in the 1994 FA Cup final against Chelsea – the only time a player has netted two spot kicks in a major English final.

Turning the clock back, Francis Lee was a prodigious penalty goalscorer for Manchester City in the late 60s and early 70s. In fact, he scored an amazing 15 spot kicks in the 1971–72 season alone.

He earned many of the kicks himself, falling to the ground after occasionally debatable contact from defenders and earning the nickname Lee Won Pen.

Despite his superb record at club level, Lee missed both the penalties he took while playing for England, smacking the crossbar against Wales (May 1969) and firing horribly wide against Portugal (December 1969).

Ron Flowers, a centre-back with Wolves in the 50s and 60s, is England's most successful international penalty-taker. He shares his six-goal haul from the spot with Alan Shearer, but unlike his modern counterpart, he never failed from 12 yards. Shearer missed once, during a World Cup qualifier in May 1997, when he hit the post against Poland.

Jan Molby netted an impressive 42 penalties for Liverpool between 1984 and 1995, but perhaps his most memorable moment came in November 1986 when he successfully converted three spot kicks in the same game against Coventry City to grab an unusual hat-trick.

Other players to have achieved this feat include Andy Blair for Sheffield Wednesday in 1984 and Kevin Dillon for Portsmouth in 1986. Henrik Larsson scored a penalty hat-trick for Sweden against Moldova in 2001 and Ronaldo repeated that feat in a World Cup qualifier for Brazil against Argentina in 2004.

Conversely, Martin Palmeiro missed three separate penalties in a single game for Argentina against Colombia during the Copa America tournament in 1999. Colombia won the game 3–0, but managed to miss a penalty themselves when Hamilton Ricard's effort was saved!

At international level, Germany and Argentina are vying for the title of Penalty Kings.

FANTASTIC FOOTBALL FACTS

Since losing 5–3 on penalties to Czechoslovakia in the 1976 European Championship final, Germany have won four major shoot-outs. At the World Cup they have beaten France (1982 semi-final), Mexico (1986 quarter-final) and England (1990 semi-final), while also emerging victorious against England in the Euro '96 semi-final.

Argentina, meanwhile, have also won three World Cup shoot-outs: Yugoslavia (1990 quarter-final), Italy (1990 semi-final) and England (1998 second round)

In the Copa America, they have knocked out Brazil (1993 quarter-final) and Colombia (1993 semi-final) on penalties and have only ever suffered one defeat in a shoot-out when they lost to Brazil at the quarter-final stage of the tournament in 1995.

Having lost three times to Germany and once to Argentina, you would think England might have picked up some tips on taking penalties. But their only success has been against Spain in the Euro '96 quarter-final.

PAYING THE PENALTY

Having a free shot at goal with just the keeper to beat from 12 yards out should be easy and yet some of the game's very best players manage to mess it up.

Missing a penalty is one thing, firing a blank when it really counts can haunt a career.

Gary Lineker

Lineker could have drawn level with Bobby Charlton as England's leading scorer on 49 goals in a friendly against Brazil in 1992, but his shot looked more like a dodgy amateur golfer with a sand wedge and was caught with ease by Brazil keeper Carlos. England also missed out on a rare win against the Brazilians as the game ended 1–1.

Dennis Bergkamp
Bergkamp should have ended Manchester United's treble dreams before they began in April 1999, but had his shot saved by Peter Schmeichel in their FA Cup semi-final replay with a few minutes left and it remained 1–1. Ryan Giggs won it for United in extra time.

Roberto Baggio
The Italian had almost single-handedly got his country to the World Cup final in 1994 only to turn from hero to zero when it mattered most. The game went to penalties after a dour 0–0 and Baggio sent Italy's final kick into orbit to gift Brazil a 3–2 win and the trophy.

Stuart Pearce and Chris Waddle
After 120 minutes had kept England and West Germany tied at 1–1 in the semi-final of the World Cup in 1990, both players chose blasting over placing during the penalty shoot-out. Pearce's effort was saved with ease, while Waddle's was more of a danger to the fans than the goal as it went high over the bar and England lost 4–3.

Michael Gray
One of the most costly misses in football's history came in the play-off final between Charlton and Sunderland in May 1998. The millionaires' playground of the Premiership was at stake and, after the game ended 4–4, Sunderland defender Gray was the odd man out in a 7–6 loss in the shoot-out.

Andy Johnson
Trevor Francis burst out crying after seeing his dreams of winning the League Cup final as Birmingham manager ruined when striker Andy Johnson failed to beat Liverpool keeper Sander Westerweld in February 2001. The game ended 1–1 and Johnson was the only player to miss in the shoot-out. Liverpool won 5–4.

FANTASTIC FOOTBALL FACTS

Terry Venables

Would have secured his place as a Barcelona legend if he had won the European Cup as manager in 1986. But his team not only failed to score in two hours of open play, they missed the target in the shoot-out and lost to unfancied Steaua Bucharest 2–0.

Arsenal 1999–2000

The Gunners notched a hat-trick no club should be proud of in the season 1999–2000 by being knocked out of the FA Cup, League Cup and the UEFA Cup in penalty shoot-outs – the latter was in the final against Galatasaray. Only Ray Parlour found the net in a crushing 4–1 loss.

Gary McAllister

There is never a good time to miss from the spot, but as a Scot playing the Auld enemy England on their home ground in the European Championships, it doesn't get much worse. McAllister had the chance to level the Euro '96 group game at 1–1, but as he ran in the ball mysteriously moved on its spot and keeper David Seaman saved his shot. The midfielder's agony was doubled moments later when Paul Gascoigne scored England's second goal to wrap up the victory.

At international level, Holland sit miserably at the bottom of the losers' table having failed to win a single shoot-out in their history. The Dutch have learned to fear the penalty spot after seeing four major championships go up in smoke – perhaps not surprising with their opponents scoring a remarkable 17 out of 18 kicks.

In the World Cup they lost to Brazil (semi-final 1998), but their agony has been mainly saved for the European Championships. Denmark (semi-final 1992), France (quarter-final 1996) and Italy (semi-final 2000) have all sent the Dutch packing.

The Italians' win against the Dutch at Euro 2000 ended a run of four consecutive shoot-out defeats. Their pain has come in the World

Cup against Argentina (semi-final 1990), Brazil (final 1994) and France (quarter-final 1998). But the rot started in the European Championship against Czechoslovakia (third/fourth place play-off 1980).

England have suffered heartbreak too. At the World Cup they lost to Germany (semi-final 1990) and Argentina (second round 1998). In the European Championships they lost to Germany again (semi-final 1996), but at least got their first victory on penalties against Spain in the previous round.

THE BEAUTIFUL GAME?

They are the players who had no chance to break sweat before running foul of the referee and gaining an unwanted place in the record books as some of the swiftest of all sendings-off.

0 secs – Swansea substitute Walter Boyd came on after 83 minutes of the goalless Division 3 match against Darlington in November 1999 after his team were awarded a free kick. Before it could be taken, Boyd clashed with Martin Gray near the penalty box, cuffed him and was dismissed. Because the referee had not restarted play, Boyd had spent zero seconds in the game.

10 secs – The world record for a sending-off after kick off involved Bologna's Giuseppe Lorenzo who struck a Parma player in an Italian League match in December 1990

13 secs – The quickest in British football was 'achieved' by Sheffield Wednesday goalkeeper Kevin Pressman, shown red for handling the ball outside the penalty area in the Division 1 match at Wolves which ended 1–1 in August 2000.

15 secs – Peterborough's Simon Rea had to go after pulling back Robert Earnshaw in the Division 2 fixture at Cardiff in November 2002 which Cardiff won 3–0.

FANTASTIC FOOTBALL FACTS

52 secs – Swindon's Ian Culverhouse received the fastest early bath in the FA Cup after handling a goal-bound effort on the line at Everton in a third-round tie which his team lost 3–0 in January 1997.

55 secs – Fastest dismissal in the World Cup was imposed on Uruguay's Jose Batista for fouling Gordon Strachan before a minute had elapsed of the match against Scotland in Neza, Mexico, in June 1986, which ended 0–0.

72 secs – Blackburn goalkeeper Tim Flowers saw red for bringing down Brian Deane at the start of the 1–1 draw against Leeds in February 1995 – the fastest Premiership dismissal.

There were some games when the referee was in danger of suffering writer's cramp, such was the number of yellow and red cards cards handed out.

18 – The most cards shown in a match at the World Cup Finals – 16 yellow and two red – were brandished by Spanish referee Antonio Lopez Nieto in Germany's 2–0 group match win over Cameroon in Shizuoka, Japan, in 2002. They were divided equally between the teams. The players dismissed for two yellows each were Carsten Ramelow, of Germany, and Cameroon's Patrick Suffo.

10 – The number of Mansfield players booked, for gross misconduct, by referee Kevin Howley for lining up at the end of an FA Cup second-round tie in November 1962 and sarcastically applauding him off for giving Crystal Palace a penalty. Only goalkeeper Colin Treharne escaped punishment. The tie ended 2–2, with Mansfield winning the replay at home 7–2.

8 – Four players from each side received their marching orders in a South American Super Cup quarter-final between Brazilian club Gremio and Penarol of Uruguay, in October 1993.

5 – Five players, all from America Tres Rios, were dismissed in the first ten minutes of a Brazilian Cup match against Itaperuna in Rio de Janeiro in November 1991 after their team conceded a disputed goal. The tie was abandoned and awarded to Itaperuna.

5 – A last-minute brawl resulted in Chesterfield's Darren Carr and Kevin Davies and Plymouth's Tony James and Richard Logan being sent packing in a Division 2 match in February 1997. Plymouth's Ron Mauge had been shown red earlier, but his team won 2–1 away from home

5 – In December 1997, incidents on the stroke of half-time brought the dismissals of David Pritchard, Jason Perry and Andy Tillson of Bristol Rovers, along with Wigan's Graeme Jones. Rovers later lost a fourth player, Josh Low, and lost the Division 2 away match 3–0.

4 – Hearts players Pasquale Bruno, David Weir, Neil Pointon and Paul Ritchie were sent off in separate second-half incidents during a Scottish Premier Division match at Ibrox which Rangers won 3–0, in September 1996.

3 – Two Premiership matches have produced three dismissals from one side. Barnsley's Darren Barnard, Chris Morgan and Darren Sheridan saw red in a 3–2 home defeat by Liverpool in March 1998 while West Ham's Shaka Hislop, Ian Wright and Steve Lomas walked during the 5–1 home defeat by Leeds in October 1999.

3 – Three substitutes were dismissed during a group match in Toulouse at the 1998 World Cup Finals. Denmark lost Miklos Molnar and Morten Wieghorst and South Africa lost Alfred Phiri. The game ended 1–1.

3 – Neil Warnock's Sheffield United finished with six men, but only three were sent off: Simon Tracey, George Santos and our old friend Suffo. Another three were 'injured' forcing the Division 1 match against West Brom, in March 2002, to be abandoned by referee Eddie Wolstenholme.

FANTASTIC FOOTBALL FACTS

Then there are the serial offenders – players who have been sent off in League and international matches more times than they might care to remember. But, as you can see, one fiery Scot is way out on his own.

21 – Willie Johnston (Rangers, West Brom, Vancouver Whitecaps, Hearts, Scotland)

13 – Roy McDonough (Birmingham, Walsall, Chelsea, Colchester, Southend, Exeter, Cambridge)

13 – Steve Walsh (Wigan, Leicester, Norwich, Coventry)

12 – Vinnie Jones (Wimbledon, Leeds, Sheffield United, Chelsea, QPR)

12 – Mark Dennis (Birmingham, Southampton, QPR)

12 – Roy Keane (Manchester United, Republic of Ireland)

12 – Dennis Wise (Wimbledon, Chelsea, Leicester, Millwall)

11 – Alan Smith (Leeds, England)

9 – Patrick Vieira (Arsenal)

Carlton Palmer was sent off with each of his five Premiership clubs – Sheffield Wednesday, Leeds, Southampton, Nottingham Forest and Coventry.

DON'T GIVE UP THE DAY JOB

Most fans, managers and players assume that referees don't have a day job – they simply drop in from outer space to make their lives a misery. But the real men in black have always had some varied and unusual careers outside football ...

Jack Taylor combined being a Wolverhampton butcher with refereeing at the top level in the 1970s. At well over six feet tall, Taylor was such a commanding figure that even Franz Beckenbauer dared not argue with him when he awarded Holland a penalty in the first minute of the 1974 World Cup final. Mind you the Germans were awarded a spot kick of their own before going on to win.

A schoolmaster at the exclusive Harrow public school might seem an unlikely job for a top referee dealing with the likes of Vinnie Jones and Roy Keane, but David Elleray was one of England's top referees during the 1990s. His aloof style upset some fans, but he took no nonsense from the players.

The common accusation aimed at refs is that they have never played at the highest level, but you could not have said that of Major Francis Marindin, who played in two FA Cup finals before going on to referee another eight in the nineteenth century. He finally became President of the FA.

You don't have to be a genius to referee, but it can help. Claude Colombo of France is one of UEFA's top refs, and is also a professor of Economic and Social Sciences. That should help when he has to lecture players on their behaviour.

Refereeing is not always a laugh a minute, but you don't have to look down in the mouth all the time. Unless, that is, you are a dentist like two of UEFA's top men, Marcus Merk and Franz Xavier Wack of Germany. Spain's Eduardo Iturralde Gonzalez goes one further – he is an orthodontist.

Many policemen become referees – it's a natural fit. But one top assistant referee in England, who prefers to remain anonymous, is not just a plain copper – he is one of the police's top marksmen, often called into sieges and hostage situations. Not a man to argue with over a dodgy offside decision.

Back in the good old days when players used to drown their sorrows in the pub, referee Jim Finney would have been a sight for sore eyes.

FANTASTIC FOOTBALL FACTS

Finney, who was in charge of the 1962 FA Cup final between Spurs and Burnley, pulled pints on days off at his pub in Hereford.

It's no surprise that 60s stalwart Roger Kirkpatrick always kept his head when in charge of big games. On his rare days off he was chief of a millinery factory.

IT'S JUST NOT CRICKET

Once the football season is over the nightmare thought of how to spend a Saturday afternoon without a match becomes reality. Here we take a look at the summer sport some footballers could have turned to were it not for the temptation of the beautiful game.

Phil Neville

The Manchester United defender had to make the tough decision over whether to play football or cricket. By the age of 14 he had represented his country at both sports. He is the youngest player to score a century for Lancashire Second XI.

Neville says: 'It wasn't even a matter of choosing, the choice was made for me. I probably wouldn't have been offered a cricket contract until the age of 18, whereas at United I was signed up at 14. I played for England at cricket and football.'

Ron Harris

A Chelsea legend who became known as 'Chopper' for his hardman image on the football field, but he could have had a more gentlemanly career on the cricket field.

Harris was a competent cricketer and had the opportunity to play for Surrey, but in the end it was money that ruled his head.

Chopper picked up £6 per game with Chelsea, but was offered just £4 an appearance for Surrey!

Geoff Hurst
England's 1966 hat-trick hero played cricket for Essex against Lancashire – making him the only first-class cricketer to have won a World Cup winners' medal. Howzat!

Denis Compton
Denis was probably the ultimate sportsman as he played at the top in both football and cricket.

Compton established himself as one of Arsenal's finest-ever players during his time at Highbury between 1936 and 1950, and also represented England and Middlesex at cricket.

Leslie Compton
The lesser-known brother of Denis also played for Arsenal and was a strong, dominant centre half. In the summer he changed sports and played as wicketkeeper for Middlesex from 1938 to 1952 – but he was far better at football.

Chris Balderstone
He made sporting history when he rushed from Leicestershire's crucial County Championship match against Derbyshire at Chesterfield to play for Doncaster Rovers in a Fourth Division showdown with Brentford.

Phil Neal
Neal used to spend his summers playing cricket with Worcester, but turned his attention to the football field with Lincoln in the winter months.

He retired from the playing side of cricket in 1986 and immediately qualified as an umpire, where he again made history. He became the first-ever third umpire to be used in a test match.

HIDDEN TALENTS

Footballers live the dream when they run out onto the pitch each week and enjoy all the trappings that come from such a lucrative career. But what would they be doing if they had not made it all the way to the top? Alternative careers beckon.

James Beattie

The Southampton and England striker only started playing football seriously after his dreams of becoming a top swimmer were threatened by injury. Beattie was the second-best swimmer in the country for his age at one stage but a shoulder problem forced him to turn his attention to football.

Beattie says: 'I did 100 metres freestyle and used to do 50 miles a week training. I was doing the swimming, going morning and evening, but then my shoulder started hurting me and a specialist said: "Your cartilage is worn away in your shoulder. You can either stop and your cartilage might grow back or you can keep going and face the consequences later on in life." So I started playing football seriously at 14 and Blackburn spotted me at school.'

Danny Dichio

The lanky forward faced the tough choice of travelling the world's top clubs as a house and garage DJ or play football. After a spell in the pirate radio scene Dichio decided to set his mind on the biggest love in his life – football.

He says: 'It was just something I enjoyed and took a bit further, a bit like football really! But football has always been my first love, no

doubt about it. I still enjoy doing it as a hobby, it's good fun but the
real trouble is that football and DJ-ing aren't so compatible really,
the healthy life and the late-night club life.'

Gareth Ainsworth
The QPR midfielder can always turn his attention to the music scene
if his career begins to go downhill. While at Wimbledon Ainsworth
set up a band with his team-mate Trond Andersen and the grounds-
man Chris Perry.

Ainsworth's mum turned down a record deal from EMI when she
was younger but Ainsworth could still use his vocal talents to make
some extra cash once his playing days are over.

Nolberto Solano
When he's not being adored by thousands of adoring Aston Villa
fans, Solano is away blowing his own trumpet – literally. The
Peruvian even used to have a recording of himself playing the trumpet as his answer phone message.

Word has it that he used to bring his trumpet into the dressing
room while at Newcastle but appearances were limited to the training ground, as boss Bobby Robson was not a fan.

Dion Dublin
The former Manchester United striker likes to spend much of his
spare time making sweet music on his saxophone. No doubt he was
delighted when Solano left Newcastle to join him at Aston Villa.

David James
From the catwalk to the American football field the England keeper
likes to strut his stuff. Past modelling deals include the likes of
Armani as his employers, while more recently he underwent an
intensive training session with the Miami Dolphins. The multi-tal-
ented shot-stopper is also a first-rate portrait artist.

Freddie Ljungberg
Back in Sweden Ljungberg built up a reputation for being a talented handball player. The Arsenal man was also good on blades and could have made a career as a professional ice hockey player.

SIZE DOESN'T MATTER
Any player will tell you, it's trophies that matter, and women are always insisting size doesn't matter. But surely they'd both rather be getting their hands on the big ones?

1. FA Premier League Trophy: 105.5cm (3ft 5.5in), 25kg (55lb)
The players say it's the league that matters, and in England it is certainly the biggest trophy on offer.

2. Intercontinental Cup: 78cm (2ft 7in), 29kg (63lb 13oz) UEFA
When the winners of the European Champions League and the South American Copa Libertadores want to know who is better, they are playing for a trophy bigger than their respective honours.

3. UEFA Champions League: 74cm (2ft 5in), 8kg (17lb 10oz) UEFA
The holy grail of trophies in Europe is surprisingly light, considering its size. Maybe the manufacturers took its holiness too literally.

4. UEFA Cup: 65cm (2ft 2in), 15kg (33lb) UEFA
Another big European trophy, somewhat devalued by having to accept all the Champions League rejects.

5. UEFA Cup-Winners' Cup: 60cm (24in), 14kg (30lb 13oz) UEFA
The now defunct trophy was never successfully retained, and having been 'retired' at the end of the 1998–99 season, will be forever retained by UEFA in a lovely cabinet in Nyon.

FANTASTIC FOOTBALL FACTS

6. European Football Championship: 50.5cm (20in), 10kg (22lb) UEFA

Another one the players love to get their hands on, the European Championships – along with the World Cup – ensure football fans only have empty summers every other year.

7. FA Cup: 48cm (19in), 5kg (175oz). (Football Association)

This solid silver number dates from the days before size mattered. It is a quality trophy even if it is a replica. The current edition is the fourth cup, having been introduced in 1992.

8. UEFA Super Cup: 42.5cm (17in), 5kg (11lb) UEFA

The Super Cup final, played between the winners of the Champions League and the UEFA cup each year, has provided many memorable matches down the years, like...

9. FIFA World Cup: 36cm (14in) 5kg (11lb) 18ct gold (FIFA)

Conclusive proof that size doesn't matter, a small trophy, but the one they all want to win. Designed by Italian artist Silvio Gazzaniga it replaced the original 'Jules Rimet trophy' for the 1974 World Cup.

   The base contains two layers of semi-precious malachite and has room for 17 small plaques bearing the name of the winners – space enough for the World Champions up to the year 2038, by which time England may have won it again!

10. Carling Cup: 27cm (11in), 3kg (105oz) (The Football League)

The only three-handled, urn-shaped trophy with sea-scroll handles and applied panels in English football. Try telling the teams that win it that it doesn't matter.

11. UEFA Intertoto Cup: 20cm (8in), 1kg (2lb 3oz) UEFA

The smallest European trophy in existence, available to footballers with small ambitions and best lifted by captains with small hands!

I'LL GET ME COAT

When a manager takes charge of a new team they set out with dreams of bringing in new players to transform falling fortunes into glory days. But things don't always work out as planned and sometimes they are out of the door almost as soon as they walk in. Here are some of the shortest spells in management ...

3 days – Bill Lambton (Scunthorpe United), 1959

7 days – Tim Ward (Exeter City), 1953

7 days – Kevin Cullis (Swansea City), 1996

10 days – Dave Cowling (Doncaster Rovers), 1997

10 days – Peter Cormack (Cowdenbeath), 2000

13 days – Johnny Cochrane (Reading), 1939

13 days – Micky Adams (Swansea City), 1997

16 days – Jimmy McIlroy (Bolton), 1970

20 days – Paul Went (Leyton Orient), 1981

27 days – Malcolm Crosby (Oxford), 1998

28 days – Tommy Docherty (QPR), 1968

32 days – Steve Coppell (Manchester City), 1996

41 days – Steve Wicks (Lincoln), 1995

44 days – Jock Stein (Leeds), 1978

44 days – Brian Clough (Leeds), 1974

48 days – John Toshack (Wales), 1994

48 days – David Platt (Sampdoria), 1999

FANTASTIC FOOTBALL FACTS

HE'S GETTING ON A BIT

The author of this book was deemed to be past-it when he tried to get a trial with Arsenal aged 18. Or maybe he was just rubbish. While it is said there are those who even think Billy Bonds is still playing for West Ham, a fair few footballers really have gone on past most recommended sell-by dates. Here are the oldest boot swingers in town.

John Ryan, owner-chairman of Doncaster Rovers, came on as a last-minute substitute in the 4–2 Conference win at Hereford in April 2003 when a week short of his 53rd birthday.

Neil McBain, aged 51 years, 120 days, kept goal for New Brighton in their 3–0 defeat at Hartlepool in a Division 3 North match in March 1947.

Stanley Matthews was 50 years, 5 days when making his last league appearance, for Stoke, in a 3–1 Division 1 victory over Fulham in February 1965.

Billy Meredith holds the record as the oldest British international, playing for Wales when 45 years, 229 days in their 2–1 win over England, in a Home International, at Highbury, in March 1920.

John Burridge was 43 years, 162 days when he played in the Premiership for Manchester City in a 3–2 home defeat by Queen's Park Rangers in May 1995.

Roger Milla, at 42 years, 39 days, became the oldest player to appear, and score, in the World Cup Finals. The match was Cameroon's 6–1 defeat by Russia in San Francisco in June 1994.

Dino Zoff captained Italy to World Cup success in July 1982 when 40 years, 92 days. His team beat West Germany 3–1 in the final in Madrid.

Gordon Strachan became the Premiership's oldest outfield player in

Coventry's 2–1 home defeat by Derby in May 1997. He was 40 years, 83 days.

IF HE'S GOOD ENOUGH, HE'S OLD ENOUGH

Fernando Rafael Garcia played for Peruvian club Juan Aurich in their 3–1 win over Estudiantes in May 2001 when 13.

Eamon Collins was 14 years, 323 days when he helped Blackpool beat Kilmarnock 2–1 in an Anglo-Scottish Cup tie in September 1980.

Derek Forster kept goal for Sunderland in a 3–3 draw against Leicester in a Division 1 match in August 1964 when 15 years, 185 days.

Gary McSheffrey set a Premiership record when, aged 16 years, 198 days, he played for Coventry in a 4–1 win at Aston Villa in February 1999.

Salomon Olembe made history as the youngest senior international at Wembley when he came on for Cameroon in their 2–0 defeat by England in November 1997 aged 16 years, 342 days.

James Milner became the youngest Premiership scorer with a goal for Leeds in their 2–1 win at Sunderland on Boxing Day 2002. He was 16 years, 357 days.

Norman Whiteside was 17 years, 41 days when first capped by Northern Ireland in a 0–0 draw against Yugoslavia in the finals of the 1982 World Cup in Zaragoza.

He holds the record as the youngest player to appear in the World Cup Finals.

Whiteside is also the youngest player to score in an FA Cup final after netting for Manchester United against Brighton in 1983 aged 18 years and 18 days.

FANTASTIC FOOTBALL FACTS

Wayne Rooney became the youngest England cap at 17 years, 111 days in the 3–1 defeat by Australia at Upton Park in February 2003.

Pele scored twice for Brazil in their 5–2 World Cup final win over Sweden in Stockholm in June 1958 when 17 years, 237 days.

Paul Allen was 17 years, 256 days when he helped West Ham beat Arsenal 1–0 in the FA Cup final at Wembley in May 1980. However, his record was broken in 2004 when Curtis Weston came off the bench for Millwall against Manchester United aged 17 years and 119 days.

WHAT A WASTE OF MONEY
The transfer market has been a salvation to some clubs, but a nightmare to most. When Blackburn owner Sir Jack Walker splashed the cash on new players in the 1990s he was rewarded with a Premiership trophy in 1995.
However, Roman Abramovich spent what seemed like billions during the 2003–04 season after buying up Chelsea and it still wasn't enough to bring silverware to Stamford Bridge.
Here are the players who have failed to live up to their massive transfer fees...

Chris Sutton
He was supposed to fire Chelsea to the Premiership title after joining the club for £10m from Blackburn in 1999. One year and one league goal later he was farmed off to Celtic for a cut-price £6m.
  Cost: £10m for one Premiership goal

Winston Bogarde
Gianluca Vialli's last signing before he was sacked as Chelsea manager in September 2000, and it was not a good leaving present.

Bogarde may have been a free transfer, but his £40,000–a-week wages paid for just two Premiership starts in four years.
   Cost: £4m per Premiership start

Ade Akinbiyi
The Nigerian international striker was so bad at Leicester, the fans dubbed him 'Ade AkinBadBuy'. Manager Peter Taylor paid Wolves £5m for his services and was rewarded with a string of embarrassing misses and just 13 goals. Akinbiyi was shipped off to Crystal Palace for £2.2m 18 months later.
   Cost: £385,000 per goal

Massimo Taibi
The Italian keeper had the unenviable task of replacing Manchester United legend Peter Schmeichel at Manchester United in 1999. He joined from Venezia for £4.5m, but made so many howlers in his first four games, boss Sir Alex Ferguson loaned him back to Italian side Reggina and he was never seen at Old Trafford again.
   Cost: £1.13m per game

Sergei Rebrov
Bought by Tottenham boss George Graham for £11m from Dynamo Kiev in June 2000 in the hope he would bring the glory days back to White Hart Lane. He arrived as one of Europe's hottest strikers, but he was farmed out on loan to Fenerbahce three years later with just 16 goals to his name and his reputation in tatters.
   Cost: £688,000 per goal

El-Hadji Diouf
Liverpool boss Gerard Houllier paid Lens £10m for the Senegal striker on the back of some impressive performances at the 2002 World Cup. But Houllier has paid the price for his judgement ever

since as Diouf has scored only six goals – a total which failed to improve in his second season despite 33 appearances.
  Cost: £1.67m per goal

Juan Sebastian Veron
Proclaimed as the best midfielder in the world by Chelsea manager Claudio Ranieri when bought for £15m from Manchester United in the summer of 2003, he looked anything but in just 11 starts in a blue shirt. Spent half the season resting a back injury at home in Argentina, while still picking up £80,000-a-week in wages.
  Cost (including wages): £1.65m per start

Steve Marlet
Bought from Lyon for £11.5m in August 2001 he became Fulham's record signing. Two years in the Premiership gave a return of just 19 goals, but it was a fall out with manager Chris Coleman that made him a hate figure among Fulham fans. Hours after promising Coleman he was staying at the club he was on a plane to complete a loan move to Marseille.
  Cost: £605,000 per goal

Robbie Fowler
At £11m, Fowler was one of the biggest signings during Leeds' days as an overspending club when he joined from Liverpool in November 2001. After scoring just 14 goals, he was sold to Manchester City 14 months later for £6m, as their cash problems began to take their toll. But even then Leeds had to continue to pay a proportion of his wages.
  Cost: £786,000 per goal

Duncan Ferguson
Newcastle paid Everton £7m for the Scot in 1998 and he was seen as the ideal partner for Alan Shearer. Ferguson spent more time on

the treatment table than the pitch however, and managed only 12 goals before Everton bought him back in 2000 for £3.75m.
  Cost: £583,000 per goal

Steve Daley
Manchester City fans were more than happy when their club snapped up experienced midfielder Daley from Wolves in September 1979, but more than a little shocked at the £1.437m transfer fee. City were in a slump and his arrival did not halt the slide and they parted company just two years later when Daley – who had netted just four goals – joined Seattle Sounders for just £300,000.
  Cost: £359,250 per goal

HOW MUCH?
What links football legends Alf Common and Zinedine Zidane? They have both been worth loads of money. From the first four-figure fee at the start of the last century, to the ridiculous Real Madrid deals, here we present an amazing transfer saga.

HOW BRITISH RECORD TRANSFERS HAVE INCREASED OVER THE YEARS

£1,000 – Alf Common, Sunderland to Middlesbrough, February 1905

£10,000 – David Jack, Bolton to Arsenal, October 1928

£100,000 – Denis Law, Manchester City to Torino, June 1961

£1,180,000 – Trevor Francis, Birmingham to Nottingham Forest, February 1979

£5.5m- David Platt, Aston Villa to Bari, July 1991

FANTASTIC FOOTBALL FACTS

£8.5m – Stan Collymore, Nottingham Forest to Liverpool, June 1995

£15m – Alan Shearer, Blackburn to Newcastle, July 1996

£29.1m – Rio Ferdinand, Leeds to Manchester United, July 2002

TOP TRANSFERS INVOLVING BRITISH CLUBS

£29.1m – Rio Ferdinand, Leeds to Manchester United, July 2002

£28.1m – Juan Sebastian Veron, Lazio to Manchester United, July 2001

£25m – David Beckham, Manchester United to Real Madrid, July 2003

£24m – Didier Drogba, Marseilles to Chelsea, July 2004

£22.5m – Nicolas Anelka, Arsenal to Real Madrid, August 1999

£22m – Marc Overmars, Arsenal to Barcelona, July 2000

£19m – Ruud van Nistelrooy, PSV Eindhoven to Manchester United, April 2001

£18m – Rio Ferdinand, West Ham to Leeds, November 2000

£17m – Damien Duff, Blackburn to Chelsea, July 2003

TOP FOREIGN SIGNINGS

£47.2m – Zinedine Zidane, Juventus to Real Madrid, July 2001

£37.2m – Luis Figo, Barcelona to Real Madrid, July 2000

£35m – Hernan Crespo, Parma to Lazio, July 2000

£33m – Ronaldo, Inter Milan to Real Madrid, August 2002

£32.6m – Gianluigi Buffon, Parma to Juventus, July 2001

£31m – Christian Vieri, Lazio to Inter Milan, June 1999

£29m – Gaizka Mendieta, Valencia to Lazio, July 2001

£28m – Rui Costa, Fiorentina to AC Milan, July 2001

FA CUP

It's the greatest knock-out competition in the world, dating back to 1872. Here are some facts and figures that are not so well-known about the FA Cup.

Only three players have ever scored hat-tricks in the final: Billy Townley for Blackburn who beat Sheffield Wednesday 6–1 in 1890; Jimmy Logan for Notts County who defeated Bolton 4–1 in 1894; and Blackpool's Stan Mortensen in their 4–3 success against Bolton in 1953.

Five pairs of brothers have played in modern-day finals – Denis and Leslie Compton for Arsenal, who beat Liverpool 2–0 in 1950; George and Ted Robledo for Newcastle who defeated Arsenal 1–0 in 1952; Ron and Allan Harris for Chelsea, beaten 2–1 by Tottenham in 1967; Jimmy and Brian Greenhoff for Manchester United, successful by 2–1 against Liverpool in 1977; Gary and Phil Neville for Manchester United, who overcame Liverpool 1–0 in 1996 and Newcastle 2–0 in 1999.

The longest round in the competition was in 1963 when bad weather meant that the third round took 66 days to complete. There were 261 postponements.

Before a maximum of one replay was introduced in 1992, there were many marathon ties. One involved Arsenal and Sheffield Wednesday who played five times before Arsenal won their third-round game 2–0 in 1979

Martin Buchan is the only player to have captained Scottish and English FA Cup-winning teams – Aberdeen who beat Celtic 3–1 in 1970 and Manchester United in their 2–1 win over Liverpool in 1977.

FANTASTIC FOOTBALL FACTS

Winger Ian Callaghan holds the record for most appearances in the competition – 88. He played in 79 matches for Liverpool, seven for Swansea and two for Crewe, collecting a winners' medal twice with Liverpool, against Leeds in 1965 (2–1) and Newcastle in 1974 (3–0)

Tottenham were banned by the FA from the 1994–95 competition for financial irregularities, but readmitted on appeal and reached the semi-finals where they lost 4–1 to Everton.

Southampton's Paul Jones became the first goalkeeper to come on as a substitute in a final, replacing the injured Antti Niemi in the 1–0 defeat by Arsenal in 2003.

Chris Baird was such an unexpected choice for Southampton in the 2003 Final against Arsenal that he did not appear in the match programme team profiles.

Yeovil Town are the greatest giant-killers of all. Before making their debut as a league club in the 2003–04 season, they had scored 20 wins over league opponents. Their finest was a 2–1 fourth-round victory over then-mighty Sunderland in 1949. Yeovil also reached the third round a record 13 times.

Dave Beasant and David Seaman have been rare examples of goalkeepers captaining winning teams in the final. Beasant led Wimbledon to their shock 1–0 win over Liverpool in 1988. Seaman skippered Arsenal to the 1–0 victory over Southampton in 2003.

Roy Keane is the only man to play in six postwar FA Cup finals. He featured for Nottingham Forest against Tottenham in 1991 and then for Manchester United against Chelsea (1994), Everton (1995), Liverpool (1996), Newcastle United (1999) and Millwall (2004). Keane has claimed four winners medals, losing just twice in the matches against Tottenham and Everton.

Joe Mercer (Arsenal 1950 and Manchester City 1969), Bob Stokoe (Newcastle 1955 and Sunderland 1973), Don Revie (Manchester City

1956 and Leeds 1972), Terry Venables (Tottenham 1967 and Tottenham 1991), George Graham (Arsenal 1971 and Arsenal 1993), Gianluca Vialli (Chelsea 1997 and Chelsea 2000) all won the FA Cup as a player before claiming the trophy as a manager. Kenny Dalglish also achieved the feat as Liverpool's player-manager in 1986.

Among the famous players never to have won the FA Cup are Tommy Lawton, Tom Finney, Johnny Haynes, Gordon Banks, George Best and Peter Shilton. Lawton, Haynes and Best never even made it to a final. Finney was a loser with Preston (2–3 v WBA) in 1954. Gordon Banks lost two finals with Leicester (0–2 v Tottenham 1961 and 1–3 v Manchester United 1963) while Shilton was in the Leicester side beaten 1–0 by Manchester City in 1969.

Winners of most finals: Manchester United with 11 (1909, 1948, 1963, 1977, 1983, 1985, 1990, 1994, 1996, 1999 and 2004).

Losers of most finals: Arsenal (L7 W9), Newcastle (L7 W6), Everton (L7 W5)

WORLD CUP

Football's biggest show on earth has embraced drama, heartbreak, tragedy and more than its fair share of unusual facts.

Ernst Willimowski scored four times for Poland against Brazil in the 1938 Finals in France and still finished a loser, his team going down 6–5.

Sixteen years before he managed England to their most famous victory at Wembley, Alf Ramsey was a member of the side that suffered one of the World Cup's biggest upsets – a 1–0 defeat by the USA in Belo Horizonte, Brazil, in 1950. When teleprinters delivered the result to newspapers in London, sports desks insisted there had been a misprint.

FANTASTIC FOOTBALL FACTS

Just Fontaine, of France, holds the record for most goals in the Finals, scoring 13 in Sweden in 1958 when his team finished third.

England's Ken Aston refereed one of the most notorious matches in World Cup history – the 1962 Battle of Santiago in which armed police came on to the field three times. He sent off two Italian players Giorgio Ferrini and Mario David, but missed their captain Huberto Maschio having his nose broken by a left hook from Chile's Leonel Sanchez. Aston was later the instigator of red and yellow cards.

The solid gold Jules Rimet Trophy was stolen while on exhibition at Central Hall, Westminster, prior to the 1966 Finals in England. It was found a few days later by a dog named Pickles under a bush in a south London garden.

Mexico, hosts in 1970, became the first country to stage the Finals twice when Colombia relinquished the 1986 tournament because of economic problems.

Two players have scored in every match of the tournament to help their teams to victory: Alcide Ghiggia for Uruguay in Brazil in 1950 and Brazil's Jairzinho in Mexico in 1970.

Argentina's Pedro Monzon became the first player to be sent off in a World Cup final. He was dismissed against West Germany in Rome in 1990 for a tackle on Jürgen Klinsmann. Team-mate Gustavo Dezotti followed in their 1–0 defeat for pushing Jürgen Kohler. The last player sent off was Marcel Desailly for a tackle on Cafu during France's 3–0 win over Brazil in Paris in 1998.

The Brazilian defender Cafu became the first player to have appeared in three World Cup finals. He came on as a substitute against Italy in the 1994 final, when Brazil won 3–2 on penalties in Los Angeles, started the 3–0 defeat by France in Paris in 1998 and led his country to a 2–0 win over Germany in Yokohama in 2002.

Hakan Sukur's goal after 11 seconds for Turkey in their 3–2 win over South Korea in the third-place play-off match in Daegu in 2002 was the fastest-ever in the finals.

Germany goalkeeper Oliver Kahn was chosen by the media as the best player in Japan and South Korea in 2002 – before the final when his mistake presented Ronaldo with Brazil's first goal in their 2–0 win in Yokohama.

CAN YOU HEAR ME AT THE BACK?

In this age of sterile all-seater stadiums people seem to get excited when gates exceed 60,000. Here are some record-breaking matches that showed how football really is the game of the masses.

World Cup record: 199,850. Brazil 1 Uruguay 2, final match, final pool, Maracana Stadium, Rio de Janeiro, July 1950.

Home international: 149,547. Scotland 3 England 1, Hampden Park, April 1937.

Scottish Cup final: 146,433. Celtic 2 Aberdeen 1, Hampden Park, April 1937.

British club match (apart from a Cup final): 143,470. Rangers 1 Hibernian 0, Scottish Cup semi-final, Hampden Park, March 1948.

European Cup: 135,826. Celtic 2 Leeds 1, semi-final second leg, Hampden Park, April 1970.

European Cup final: 127,621. Real Madrid 7 Eintracht Frankfurt 3, Hampden Park, May 1960.

FA Cup final: 126,047. Bolton 2 West Ham 0, Wembley, April 1923.

World Cup qualifying tie: 120,000. Cameroon 2 Morocco 1, Yaounde, November 1981.

FANTASTIC FOOTBALL FACTS

Scottish League: 118,567. Rangers 2 Celtic 1, Ibrox Park, January 1939.

Football League: 83,260. Manchester United 1 Arsenal 1, Maine Road, January 1948.

Premiership: 67,758. Manchester United 3 Southampton 2, Old Trafford, January 2004.

YOU'RE SUPPOSED TO BE AT HOME/IS THAT ALL YOU TAKE AWAY?

More people watch the World Cup on television than they do the Olympic Games, it is claimed. But that does not mean people can always be persuaded to get off their backsides and fork out a few quid to go and watch a game in the flesh. Loyal supporters? Some of you should be ashamed. Here are the matches that recorded the lowest-ever attendances.

Football League:13
Stockport 0 Leicester 0, Division 2, May 1921 (at Old Trafford – Stockport ground closed).

Scottish League Cup: 29
Clydebank 1 East Stirling 2, 1st round, July 1999 (at shared ground – Morton).

International (modern day): 221
Poland 4 Northern Ireland 1, friendly, February 2002 (in Limassol, Cyprus – Poland World Cup base).

Football League (postwar): 450
Rochdale 0 Cambridge 2, Division 3, February 1974.

League Cup: 612
Halifax 1, Tranmere 2, 1st round 2nd leg, September 2000.

Football League (new format): 849
Wimbledon 2 Rotherham 1, Division 1, October 2002.

International at home (modern day): 2,315
Wales 3 Northern Ireland 0, Home International, May 1982,
Wrexham.

England match (post war): 2,378
San Marino 1 England 7, World Cup qualifier, November 1993 (in
Bologna)

Premiership: 3,039
Wimbledon 1 Everton 3, January 1993.

Top division at major ground (postwar): 4,554
Arsenal 0 Leeds 3, May 1966 (clashed with TV coverage of Cup-
Winners' Cup final, Liverpool v Borussia Dortmund).

GOING DOWN

Relegation may well be the dirtiest word in football and a fate that all clubs and fans would rather avoid. However, some clubs are better than others at avoiding the drop and putting their supporters through that particular nightmare.

Notts County hold the record for the most relegated side in English league football having gone down on no fewer than 15 occasions in their history. However, they have also earned promotion 11 times, so at least the fans do not have to suffer too many seasons of mid-table mediocrity with no excitement!

Grimsby are next in the relegation stakes having dropped 14 times, including back-to-back relegations in 2002–03 and 2003–04 to end up in Division Three.

Bolton Wanderers may enjoy an illustrious history, but they have found themselves demoted 12 times.

Birmingham City have had plenty of highs and lows over the years and it is perhaps no surprise that they have been relegated on 12 occasions.

Since their heyday in the 1960s, Manchester City have bounced up and down the divisions like a rubber ball. In their entire history the club have suffered 12 relegations – putting them at number five in the all-time list – but have also enjoyed 11 promotions.

Conversely, perennial under-achievers Rochdale have rarely given their fans much to worry about or get excited about. The Lancashire club have been stuck in the bottom division for the majority of their time in the league and have actually suffered just two relegations.

Arsenal are another club unaccustomed to the drop. The Gunners have only been relegated once in their history and have been in the top flight of English football for the longest unbroken spell – since 1919.

MOST RELEGATED PLAYERS

While some teams have icons – players that can inspire the team when the chips are down – others seem keen to take on albatrosses – players who bring bad luck wherever they go.

Just take a look at this list of footballers for whom relegation from the Premiership has become a habit!

Nathan Blake – Sheffield United 93–94, Bolton 95–96, Blackburn 98–99, Wolverhampton Wanderers 03–04

Paul Dickov – Manchester City 00–01, Leicester City 01–02, Leicester City 03–04

Benito Carbone – Sheffield Wednesday 99–00, Bradford 00–01, Derby County 01–02

Des Lyttle – Nottingham Forest 96–97, 98–99, Watford 99–00, West Brom 02–03

Hermann Hreidarsson – Crystal Palace 97–98, Wimbledon 99–00, Ipswich 01–02

Jan-Aage Fjortoft – Swindon Town 93–94, Middlesbrough 96–97, Barnsley 97–98

Alex Rae – Sunderland 96–97, Wolverhampton Wanderers 03–04

Mark Kennedy – Manchester City 00–01, Wolverhampton Wanderers 03–04

Les Ferdinand – West Ham 02–03, Leicester 03–04

Carlton Palmer – Nottingham Forest 98–99, Coventry 00–01

Neil Redfearn – Barnsley 97–98, Charlton 98–99

Dougie Freedman – Crystal Palace 97–98, Nottingham Forest 98–99

Tim Flowers – Blackburn 98–99, Leicester City 01–02

Christian Dailly – Blackburn 98–99, West Ham 02–03

Jason McAteer – Blackburn 98–99, Sunderland 02–03

Neil Cox – Bolton 97–98, Watford 99–00

Marcus Bent – Crystal Palace 97–98, Ipswich 01–02

Georgiou Kinkladze – Manchester City 95–96, Derby County 01–02

Alan Rogers – Nottingham Forest 96–97, Leicester City 01–02

Brian Deane – Leicester City 01–02, West Ham 02–03

Lee Carsley – Blackburn 98–99, Coventry 00–01

Ian Nolan – Sheffield Wednesday 99–00, Bradford 00–01

Dean Saunders – Nottingham Forest 96–97, Bradford 00–01

Alf-Inge Haaland – Nottingham Forest 96–97, Manchester City 00–01

Trevor Sinclair – QPR 95–96, West Ham 02–03

Gary Breen – Coventry 00–01, West Ham 02–03

Steve Lomas – Manchester City 95–96, West Ham 02–03

Marcus Stewart – Ipswich 01–02, Sunderland 02–03

Mart Poom – Derby County 01–02, Sunderland 02–03

Ashley Ward – Barnsley 97–98, Blackburn 98–99, Bradford 00–01

FANTASTIC FOOTBALL FACTS

Gerry Taggart – Bolton 97–98, Leicester 01–02

Neil Shipperley – Crystal Palace 97–98, Nottingham Forest 98–99

Fabrizio Ravanelli – Middlesbrough 96–97, Derby County 01–02

Tony Coton – Manchester City 95–96, Sunderland 96–97

MORE CLUBS THAN NICKLAUS

Footballers are a notoriously loyal bunch of badge kissers who love their clubs like fans and feel that playing for another club would be like cheating on their wives … yeah right!

The following players probably think loyalty means gaining points on their store card while shopping.

31 – John Burridge (1970–1997) comes in at number one having made appearances for 15 clubs – Workington, Blackpool, Aston Villa, Southend United, Crystal Palace, Queen's Park Rangers, Wolverhampton Wanderers, Derby County, Sheffield United, Southampton, Newcastle United, Scarborough, Lincoln City, Manchester City and Darlington.

He also made Scottish League appearances for five clubs – Hibernian, Aberdeen, Falkirk, Dumbarton and Queen of the South.

Not only that but he had spells with Hartlepool United, Notts County, Grimsby Town and Northampton Town, but made no League appearances for them.

He was also at Dunfermline Athletic (but made no appearances) and had spells outside the League with Enfield, Witton Albion, Gateshead, Durham City, Purfleet and Blyth Spartans – an amazing 31 clubs in total.

19 – Mark Prudhoe (1981–2003) appeared for 14 clubs including Sunderland, Hartlepool United, Birmingham City, Walsall, Doncaster Rovers, Grimsby Town, Bristol City, Carlisle United,

Darlington, Stoke City, Peterborough United, York City, Bradford City and Southend United.

He also signed but didn't play for another five – Sheffield Wednesday, Liverpool, Darlington, Bradford and Macclesfield.

15 – Barry Siddall (1971–1994) played for Bolton, Sunderland, Darlington, Port Vale, Stoke, Tranmere, Manchester City, Blackpool, Stockport, Hartlepool, West Brom, Carlisle, Chester City, Preston North End and Bury.

14 – Brett Angell (1986–2003) got to see a lot of the country thanks to spells at QPR, Port Vale, Rushden, Walsall, Preston North End, Notts County, West Brom, Sheffield United, Sunderland, Everton, Southend United, Stockport County, Derby and Portsmouth.

14 – Phil Kite (1980–1996) managed to play for both Bristol City and Bristol Rovers, but also crammed in Cardiff, Stockport, Crewe, Rotherham, Plymouth, Mansfield, Sheffield United, Bournemouth, Gillingham, Middlesbrough, Southampton and Tottenham.

13 – Lee Chapman (1978–1996) played for Swansea, Leeds (twice), Ipswich, Southend, West Ham, Portsmouth, Nottingham Forest, Niort, Sheffield Wednesday, Sunderland, Arsenal, Plymouth and Stoke.

13 – Winston White (1977–1993) made it a lucky 13 by playing for Leicester City, Hereford United, Chesterfield, Port Vale, Stockport County, Bury, Rochdale, Colchester United, Burnley, West Brom, Carlisle United, Doncaster Rovers and Wigan Athletic.

13 – Neil Redfearn (1982–2004) played for, and more often than not got relegated with, Rochdale, Boston United, Halifax, Wigan, Bradford, Charlton, Barnsley, Oldham, Watford, Crystal Palace, Doncaster, Lincoln and Bolton.

12 – Steve Claridge (1984–2004) picked up a wage packet and boosted the bookmakers profits at Weymouth (twice), Millwall,

113

FANTASTIC FOOTBALL FACTS

Portsmouth (twice), Wolves, Leicester, Birmingham, Cambridge (twice), Luton, Aldershot, Crystal Palace, Bournemouth and Fareham Town.

11 – Terry Curran (1974–1986) was often on the move as he featured for Doncaster Rovers, Nottingham Forest, Bury, Derby, Southampton, Sheffield Wednesday, Sheffield United (twice), Everton, Huddersfield, Panionis and Hull City.

ONE-CLUB WONDERS

Some players have made a living out of regular transfer deals, but an increasingly rare number remain loyal to the cause, and not just because they normally get a testimonial match after ten years service. They are the One-Club Wonders.

Tom Finney – Preston North End
Signed for Preston in 1936 as a 14–year-old and turned professional just four years later. He retired in 1960 with his Preston career spanning 24 years. Finney played 433 games and scored 187 goals for his club.

Paolo Maldini – AC Milan
Signed as a youth player in 1984 for AC Milan and is still playing for the same club 20 years later. Has played over 600 games, but has scored less than 30 goals for his club. He has played 125 of those matches in Europe alone.

Tony Adams – Arsenal
The former England defender was at Arsenal for 20 years, playing 673 games before he started his managerial career at Wycombe Wanderers. His longevity at the club also entitled him to a rare two testimonial matches. Only David O'Leary, who finished his career at Leeds, played more games for Arsenal.

Matt Le Tissier – Southampton
Signed for the Saints in 1985 and retired in 2002 to become a living legend at his home club. He had offers to go to bigger clubs, but stayed loyal to play in 550 games, scoring 210 goals.

Jason Dodd- Southampton
Signed for Southampton in 1989 as a teenager from Bath City and was still hanging in there at the end of the 2003–04 season with nearly 500 appearences to his credit.

Ryan Giggs – Manchester United
Giggsy has been flying down the wing at Old Trafford since he signed in December 1990 and was still going strong at the end of the 2003–04 season with well over 500 appearances for the Red Devils.

Ray Parlour – Arsenal
'Ooh ah Ray Parlour.' The combative midfielder has been gunning away for Arsenal since 1991 and still hasn't had a testimonial match!

Jack Charlton – Leeds United
Although now an honorary Irishman after his management of the ROI national team, he is also a legend at Leeds having spent 21 years at the club, making 772 appearances and scoring 95 goals.

ON THE BEER
Beer and football is a match made in heaven and many cash-strapped clubs have turned their hands to a local brew in order to get some much-needed funds for the club. Here are the most magnificent seven pints you can buy, safe in the knowledge you are doing your local club a favour in the process.

FANTASTIC FOOTBALL FACTS

Luton Town
The Bedfordshire club's supporters got together with local brewers Banks and Taylor to make a light ale called Goalden Hatter.

Darlington
Liddles' Best is the official supporters' beer of the Third Division side.

Norwich City
It is said that after a hard day slaving over the stove, celebrity chef and Norwich director Delia Smith likes nothing better than to relax with a pipe and a pint of 'On The Ball', brewed by the local Humpty Dumpty brewery in Reepham.

Exeter City
The Grecian Ale has been produced by Sharp's of Wadebridge and the Exeter City's Supporters Trust benefits from a percentage of the cash from every pint sold to thirsty supporters.

Ducket Ale
Is the beer of choice for fans of Berwick Rangers and made by Border Breweries. They are the only English club that plays in the Scottish football league and their beer is named after a stand in the ground.

Forever Bury Beer
Leyden Breweries of Nangreaves brew this local delight for the fans of ... Bury. This is another brewery that donates a percentage of sales to the cash-strapped club.

Notts County
To help club fundraising efforts in the 2002–2003 season a local Nottingham brewery created a beer called Magpies Ale and it was on sale in various Nottingham pubs for a couple of months.

HAVING A LAUGH
Professional football teams are not only a talented group of men with skills on the pitch, but also a bunch of mates with a lot of time on their hands. The end result is banter, pranks and a whole heap of trouble, especially if you played for Wimbledon during the 80s.

Barnsley
When former full-back John Beresford joined the club he was told there would be a small traditional drinks reception at the start of the season. Team-mate Steve Agnew informed the new lad that the party was a fancy-dress affair and showed off his policeman's uniform.

Beresford took the bait and got himself a full clown's outfit, but the laughter soon stopped when the Lord Mayor turned up to greet the team at their full civic reception!

Newcastle
Beresford made sure he learned from that and while he was at Newcastle he once covered Lee Clark's BMW in flour.

Instead of driving away and letting it all blow off, Clark decided to wash it. The flour turned to dough and eventually hardened, ruining the classy motor.

Colombian superstar Faustino Asprilla found things a little confusing when he arrived on Tyneside. Kevin Keegan would sometimes hold training sessions at St James' Park and sometimes at the training ground. Tino thought he could rely on Mr Reliable, Alan Shearer, and would always ask him where it was. Even Shearer couldn't resist the easy catch, giving the wrong answer every time. Asprilla would turn up 45 minutes late to every session – no doubt collecting a mandatory fine each time.

Raith Rovers
Known as the Scottish Crazy Gang, Raith managed to orchestrate a three-week wind-up, with midfielder Peter Hetherston falling for it hook, line and sinker.

FANTASTIC FOOTBALL FACTS

Peter got a fake letter telling him that top TV detective show Taggart wanted him to appear in a guest role as a Glasgow footballer.

He recalls: 'The fee was for £600 but would go up to £900 if I agreed to appear nude in a shower scene. I had to get permission from Jimmy Nicholl, who was in on it all along.

'I couldn't believe it, £900 and I'd be on the telly too. I kept gearing up for my big day and this went on for three weeks, with me practising my accent and everything, until they finally let on that I'd been had.'

Wimbledon

While new striker John Hartson was putting pen to paper on a six-year deal following his £7·5 million move from West Ham, his new team-mates hung his designer Fila tracksuit out of the changing-room window at the training ground and set it ablaze. Adding to the ritual and just to rub it in, Hartson was then thrown into a puddle for good measure.

Eric Young used to bring his old Brighton kit in every day, in his Cup final bag, and he used to have the same old stuff in it. Alan Cork remembers, 'It was horrible, so one day we performed a ritual burning in the dressing-room.' Simple as that.

Dave Bassett led unfashionable Wimbledon into the top flight, enduring many insults from his detractors and pranks from his players. On one occasion, on the train home from an away match, his shoes were hurled out of the window at Watford, his scheduled stop. Bassett, pinned under a table, was unable to join them and had to proceed on to London barefooted!

Alan Cork, who signed from Derby in January 1978 and still holds the club scoring record, enjoyed a prank, saying: 'We were staying in an Army camp in Germany when an announcement came over the loudspeaker saying: "In the event of a nuclear warning, sound alarm, please put on the gas mask provided and leave the building immediately."

'We were all in on it except John Fashanu. Anyway, we let off the alarm at 5 a.m. and we're all pretending to be dying through gas. Fash dives out of bed, puts on the gas mask and all you could see was him running down the road.'

Former skipper Robbie Earle oversaw his fair share of pranks too. He said: 'By way of a gentle introduction to the club, one of our signings, Carl Leaburn, had his clothes cut to shreds. Then there was the fire in the dressing room, when Kenny Cunningham's shoes were incinerated for being unfashionable.'

Liverpool
Striker Robbie Fowler cut up a pair of Neil Ruddock's £300 Gucci shoes, after being told that the hardman had urinated in his shoes. Ruddock punched him in the nose in the middle of a crowded airport, although Steve Harkness later owned up to being the peeing prankster.

Gazza
No chapter concerning practical jokes could ever be complete without referring to the footballer's clown-in-chief, Paul Gascoigne.

On his first night in Rome after signing for Lazio, Gazza gave his minder the slip, left his shoes by an open window and hid in a cupboard – leaving the minder panicking that the club's new star had committed suicide.

While at Rangers, he took a documentary team to a beautiful Scottish cottage which he informed them was his new place. He pretended he'd forgotten his key and knocked instead. The door was dutifully opened by a befuddled housewife, at which point Gazza pretended he was filming a TV advert and asked if she preferred Daz or Omo.

In celebration of his new-found hero status after Italia '90, Gascoigne flew home wearing a huge pair of plastic boobs and stomach, bearing the legend 'Gazza'.

FANTASTIC FOOTBALL FACTS

The 'daft-as-a-brush' midfielder walked into the Middlesbrough team canteen wearing nothing but his training socks and ordered lunch.

Gazza has also been the victim of a practical joke. At Everton, team-mate Danny Cadamarteri taped Gazza's suit to the roof of his convertible Mercedes and spray-painted a body round it. While the suit was easily removed, the paint was not.

YOU'RE AN EMBARRASSMENT

A World Cup is usually a perfect excuse for mass boozing sessions followed by a bit of football – and that's just for the players. But occasionally players take things a bit too far – a stray punch here, a banned substance there – and leave their coaches no option but to boot them out in shame.

2002 – Just two weeks before the World Cup kicks off Ireland captain Roy Keane storms out of his side's World Cup training camp in Saipan, branding their preparations amateurish. After a blazing row with coach Mick McCarthy, the petulant Manchester United midfielder is put in his place by being shipped home before the tournament starts.

2002 – Uncapped Portuguese midfielder Daniel Kenedy is sent home from the World Cup in the Far East after failing a drugs test during their warm-up in May. A banned diuretic was found in the Maritimo man's system.

2000 – Glasgow Rangers midfielder Tugay has a bust-up with Turkish national manager Mustafa Denizli at Euro 2000 and is told to leave the tournament.

1998 – South African duo Naughty Mokoena and star midfielder Brendan Augustine are sent home from France '98 after arriving back at their hotel at 5 a.m. following a night of partying, despite being given a strict 10 p.m. curfew.

1996 – Dutch midfielder Edgar Davids is sent home from the European Championship in England by Dutch manager Guus Hiddink for publicly criticising the manager.

1994 – After scoring a marvellous goal against Greece in USA '94, Argentine legend Diego Maradona tests positive for ephedrine following a match with Nigeria and is thrown out of the tournament.

1994 – German midfielder Steffen Effenberg is thrown out of the national squad by manager Berti Vogts after making an obscene gesture to a section of German fans while being substituted against South Korea.

1994 – Romanian Ioan Valdoiu is sent off for an appalling foul on Stephane Chapuisat only four minutes after coming on as a substitute against Switzerland. The Romanian football federation are so incensed by the tackle they send their player home.

1978 – Scottish winger Willie Johnston tests positive for drugs after the defeat by Peru at the World Cup in Argentina and is sent home. He never plays for Scotland again.

And one referee ...

In 1994 Swiss whistler Kurt Rothlisberger is sent home by FIFA after failing to award Belgium a penalty in their second-round defeat by Germany.

A FIST FULL OF FOOTBALLERS

We all love watching a good fight. And thankfully footballers seem happy to provide one. Whether it's a case of frustrations boiling over in the heat of battle or the result of a long-standing feud, it's always enjoyable to see players going at it toe-to-toe – especially when they are on the same team. Seconds out . . .

1. Hartson v Berkovic – October 1998
West Ham striker John Hartson is filmed on camera landing a kick on the head of team-mate Eyal Berkovic during a training-ground bust-up.

2. Le Saux v Batty – November 1995
Blackburn pair Graeme Le Saux and David Batty square up during an ill fated Champions League game in Moscow. The match ended 3–0 to Spartak.

3. Sheringham v Cole – 1998 to present
The strikers refused to speak to each other during much of their time at Manchester United after Teddy Sheringham blamed Andy Cole for a goal conceded in a match against Bolton.

4. Fowler v Ruddock – September 1995
The two Liverpool players come to blows on a return flight from a UEFA Cup defeat in Moscow after Neil 'Razor' Ruddock blamed Robbie Fowler for vandalising his expensive shoes.

FANTASTIC FOOTBALL FACTS

5. Ravanelli v Cox – May 1997
The Middlesbrough pair are seen scuffling outside their team's hotel before the FA Cup final. Fabrizio Ravanelli is rumoured to be angry after Neil Cox is quoted as saying the Italian is not worth his place in the starting line up.

6. Grobbelaar v McManaman – September 1993
Bruce Grobbelaar and team-mate Steve McManaman come to blows in the Reds' penalty area during a Merseyside defeat to Everton.

7. Hogg v Levein – September 1994
During a pre-season friendly versus Raith, Hearts' Graeme Hogg has a fight with team-mate Craig Levein. Both are suspended for ten matches by the Scottish FA as a result.

8. Kiely v Todd – October 2001
Defender Andy Todd thumps keeper Dean Kiely during a training-ground argument at Charlton. Todd is later transfer-listed and leaves the club.

9. Shearer v Gillespie – 1997
A drunken Gillespie takes a swing at Shearer after a night out during a break in Dublin. Gillespie misses his target but as usual Shearer does not as he lands a punch on the Irish winger.

10. Flanagan v Hales – January 1979
Mike Flanagan and Derek Hales get mild-mannered Charlton in the list for the second time after they are sent off for fighting each other during a third-round FA Cup tie.

HE MUST BE ON DRUGS
The performance of a footballer can vary from the sublime to the ridiculous, so much so that you can often be left wondering, 'What

is he on?'. For the most part, fortunately, they're on nothing, but not always ...

Rio Ferdinand (2003–04)
Manchester United's £30m defender 'forgot' to attend a routine drugs test after training and was banned for eight months despite an appeal.

Billy Kenny (April 1994)
The former England Under-21 international was kicked out of Everton after twice testing positive for drugs under the club's own testing programme.

Paul Merson (November 1994)
Admitted to cocaine and alcohol addiction and was ordered by the FA to spend six weeks in a rehabilitation clinic.

Lee Bowyer (March 1995)
Suspended by Charlton after testing positive for cannabis.

Chris Armstrong (March 1995)
Tested positive for cannabis and was left out of four Crystal Palace games on instruction of the FA.

David Hillier (March 1995)
Suspended by Arsenal for six matches after testing positive for cannabis.

Roger Stanislaus (February 1996)
Banned for one year and subsequently sacked by his club Leyton Orient after being found guilty of using cocaine.

FANTASTIC FOOTBALL FACTS

Craig Whitington (April 1996)
The Huddersfield striker was banned by the FA for six months and sacked by his club after becoming the first English player to test positive twice for the banned substance cannabis.

Jamie Stuart (December 1997)
Kicked out by Charlton after testing positive for cocaine and marijuana.

Shane Nicholson (February 1998)
Sacked by West Brom and handed a lifetime ban (which was subsequently lifted) by the FA after failing to submit to a random drugs test.

Harry Gregg (1960s)
The former Manchester United keeper told BBC 1's Real Story programme that stimulants such as speed were widely used in the 60s, before there were any anti-doping laws. Gregg said: 'There was an expression around the game at that time – you get pills to put you to sleep, you get pills to wake you up, you get pills to dry you out.'

Yegor Titov (January 2004)
Russian midfielder Yegor Titov was banned by UEFA for 12 months after testing positive for the banned anabolic steroid nandrolone following a European Championship play-off qualifier against Wales.

Russia won the match and Wales appealed that they should take their place in the tournament, but the challenge was ultimately unsuccessful.

Mohammed Kallon (January 2004)
Inter Milan striker Mohammed Kallon tested positive for the banned anabolic steroid nandrolone and was handed an eight-month ban.

Mark Bosnich (February 2003)
Chelsea goalkeeper Mark Bosnich was banned for nine months after testing positive for cocaine.

Jaap Stam (October 2001)
The Italian FA banned Lazio's Jaap Stam for five months after he tested positive for nandrolone.

Edgar Davids (May 2001)
Edgar Davids had a five-month ban reduced to four after also testing positive for nandrolone while at Juventus.

Josep Guardiola (November 2001)
Brecia's Josep Guardiola failed a nandrolone drugs test and was subsequently banned for four months.

Fernando Couto (January 2001)
Lazio defender Fernando Couto was handed a 10-month suspension after being found guilty of taking nandrolone. However, on appeal his ban was reduced to four months.

Frank de Boer (March 2001)
Frank de Boer had a one-year ban reduced to three months on appeal having tested positive for nandrolone.

Theo Zagorakis (June 2001)
Theo Zagorakis blamed too much sex for his positive nandrolone test while at AEK Athens. His excuse was accepted and he escaped a suspension.

Christophe Dugarry (June 1999)
Christophe Dugarry also avoided a ban despite testing positive for nandrolone. The Marseille striker was set to be suspended for six

months, but played on after it was agreed that testing procedures were not properly applied.

FOOTBALLERS BEHAVING BADLY

Footballers are under the spotlight throughout their careers and when things go wrong their shame is splashed across all the papers for everyone to see. Here are some of the more infamous results of footballers behaving badly.

John Terry
The England defender was charged with affray and assault after an alleged nightclub fight involving a member of staff and two customers at the Wellington Club in central London.

John Terry – Again!
Terry was one of four Chelsea players fined by the club over a drinking binge at a hotel packed with American tourists 24 hours after the US terrorist attacks. Frank Lampard, Jody Morris, Eidur Gudjohnsen and Terry were alleged to have been swearing and vomiting at the hotel near Heathrow airport, where Americans stranded by flight cancellations were staying.

Jonathan Woodgate and Lee Bowyer
They appeared in Hull Crown Court for an alleged attack on an Asian youth. Woodgate was found guilty of affray and given 100 hours community service. Bowyer was cleared of all charges.

Kieron Dyer, Craig Bellamy, Carl Cort and Andy Griffin
All four were sent home in disgrace from the club's training camp in Marbella after they missed a function to honour former chairman Sir John Hall in order to go out drinking. The booze ended up costing them a fortune as they were all fined two weeks' wages.

Dennis Wise
In 1990 he was fined £200 and given a one-year driving ban after refusing to provide a breath specimen when stopped by police. Wise went one better a few years later by gaining a conviction, later overturned on appeal, for assaulting a London cabbie.

Ray Parlour
He had to be dropped from the England Under-21 squad because of facial injuries sustained in November 94. The midfielder sustained a fractured cheekbone and gashed face requiring four stitches in a bar-room fracas at a Sussex holiday camp. One year later he was fined £170 by Hong Kong magistrates and dropped from the England Under-21 squad again after assaulting a taxi driver.

Roy Keane
The mild-mannered midfielder was escorted from a Manchester nightclub for 'abusive behaviour' in 1994 – allegedly spitting beer at other customers and swearing. Two years later he was barred from his local Cheshire pub for life for repeated drunken behaviour.

Tony Adams
Adams spent 57 days in Chelmsford Open Prison in 1991 after being convicted of drink-driving when he drove his car into a garden wall. It was joked that he complained about the size of his cell and asked for the walls to be moved back a full ten yards.

Duncan Ferguson
Ferguson was banned for 12 matches by the SFA for head-butting Raith Rovers defender John McStay in 1993. He also served 44 days in Glasgow's Barlinnie jail for the assault. The ban was later quashed by a Scottish court.

FANTASTIC FOOTBALL FACTS

Stan Collymore
Bad-boy Collymore is now more famous as a rogue than as a footballer and was forced to make a public apology after punching TV presenter Ulrika Jonsson in a Paris bar during the 1998 World Cup. He was also sent home by Leicester City for setting off a fire extinguisher while in the Spanish resort of La Manga and, most recently, was splashed across the tabloids when caught 'dogging' – the act of having public sex with random strangers in car parks.

LAGS XI
Footballers sometimes grab the headlines for all the wrong reasons by swapping the changing room for the court-room. Here are a selection of players whose defence was not good enough to keep them out of jail. . .

Graham French
The Luton winger was imprisoned for three years in July 1990 for his part in a shooting in a Dunstable pub car park.

Graham Rix
Chelsea's assistant manager was jailed for 12 months in 1999 after being convicted of indecent assault and having unlawful sex with a 15-year-old girl.

Ronnie Mauge
While at Fulham the midfielder was sentenced to nine months imprisonment in October 1988 for assaulting his girlfriend and a bus driver.

Peter Swan
The Sheffield Wednesday and England defender was jailed for four

months in 1965 for conspiracy to defraud in a football betting scandal.

Mickey Thomas
A former Welsh international, Thomas was jailed for 18 months in July 1993 after being convicted of passing forged banknotes.

George Best
The Manchester United and Northern Ireland legend was sentenced to three months in prison for drink-driving, assaulting a policeman and jumping bail in December 1984.

Jamie Lawrence
The tricky winger, mostly remembered for his crazy hairstyles while at Bradford City, served a four-year prison sentence after being convicted of armed robbery before he embarked on his professional career.

Ricky Otto
The former Birmingham and Leyton Orient winger was jailed for four years as a teenager for robbery. He was released on remission for good behaviour after three years.

Peter Storey
Storey, a former Arsenal and England defender was jailed for 28 days in 1990 for attempting to import porn videos. He was also convicted of manufacturing fake gold coins and keeping a brothel.

Stig Tofting
The Bolton midfielder was sentenced to four months in prison by a court in Copenhagen after assaulting the manager of Café Ketchup in the Danish capital in the summer of 2002.

FANTASTIC FOOTBALL FACTS

ONE–CAP WONDERS

ENGLAND

They were often stars at club level, but these players failed to impress on the international stage, or found the competition for places just too hot. Presented here for one last bow, in alphabetical order, they are the England footballers known as the 'One–Cap Wonders'.

Jeff Blockley (Arsenal) v Yugoslavia at Wembley, 1–1, friendly, October 1972

Peter Davenport (Nottingham Forest) v Republic of Ireland at Wembley, 2–1, friendly, March 1985

Charlie George (Derby) v Republic of Ireland, at Wembley, 1–1, friendly, September 1976

Paul Goddard (West Ham) v Iceland, in Reykjavik, 1–1, friendly, June 1982

Colin Harvey (Everton) v Malta in Valletta, 1–0, European Championship qualifier, February 1971

John Hollins (Chelsea) v Spain at Wembley, 2–0, friendly, May 1967

Brian Little (Aston Villa) v Wales at Wembley, 2–2, Home International, May 1975

Brian Marwood (Arsenal) v Saudi Arabia, in Riyadh, 1–1, friendly, November 1988

Steve Perryman (Tottenham) v Iceland in Reykjavik, 1–1, friendly, June 1982

Neil Ruddock (Liverpool) v Nigeria, at Wembley, 1–0, friendly, November 1994

Tommy Smith (Liverpool) v Wales, at Wembley, 0–0, Home International, May 1971

Alex Stepney (Manchester United) v Sweden, at Wembley, 3–1, friendly, May 1968

Alan Sunderland (Arsenal) v Australia, in Sydney, 2–1, friendly, May 1980

David Unsworth (Aston Villa) v Japan, at Wembley, 2–1, friendly, June 1995

Mark Walters (Rangers) v New Zealand, in Auckland, 1–0, friendly, June 1991

Meanwhile, the other Home Nations are not so fortunate when it comes to the abundance of talent, so plenty of lower-league journeymen can amass a nice selection of tassled caps.

NORTHERN IRELAND

David Healy (2000–2004) 33 caps
Had only made one sub appearance at Manchester United when he played his first international game, scoring two goals on debut against Luxembourg.

Phil Mulryne (1997–2004) 23 caps
Made just one Premiership appearance as an apprentice at Manchester United and won all of these caps while playing in Division 1 with Norwich.

Steve Morrow (1990–2000) 39 caps
Made as many Northern Ireland appearances as he did starts for Arsenal in a nine-year spell in north London.

FANTASTIC FOOTBALL FACTS

Alan Fettis (1992–99) 25 caps
The goalkeeper was passed between 10 clubs, but still won 25 caps for his country.

SCOTLAND

Craig Burley (1995–2004) 46 caps
Still most famous for being George's nephew after unspectacular spells at Chelsea, Celtic, Derby, Dundee, Preston and Walsall.

Colin Calderwood (1995–2000) 36 caps
A regular in the Scotland side despite a series of miserable seasons at Tottenham.

Gordon Durie (1988–98) 43 caps
'Jukebox' netted the majority of his club goals in Scotland, which never helped Chris Sutton get in the England team.

Eoin Jess (1993–99) 18 caps
Netted 80 goals in two spells at Aberdeen, but found life much harder down in England with Coventry, Bradford and Nottingham Forest.

David Weir (1997–2004) 37 caps
Plodding on at Everton helped Weir to this impressive haul of international appearances.

WALES

Paul Bodin (1990–95) 23 caps
Would impressing at Cardiff, Swindon and Reading have earned Bodin 23 caps if he'd been English?

Barry Horne (1988–97) 59 caps
For making a career out of kicking people up in the air, Horne won as many Welsh caps as Peter Beardsley and Des Walker did for England.

Darren Barnard (1998–2004) 21 caps
Barnard failed to make much of an impact at Chelsea, but that didn't stop him racking up the appearances for Wales.

Andrew Melville (1990–2004) 63 caps
Successive Welsh managers were unconcerned that Melville was never blessed with much pace as he remained a permanent fixture in the national team.

ALL-TIME FANTASY LEFT-FOOTED XI
Coaches are sometimes obsessed with getting the balance of their team right, and in England's case often struggle to find left-footed players.

   But here we have selected a team of left-footed talent from the all-time greats.

Fabien Barthez
(French)

Roberto Carlos   **Christien Chivu**   **Frank de Boer**   **Paolo Maldini**
(Brazilian)   (Romanian)   (Dutch)   (Italian)

Johan Cruyff   **Ferenc Puskas**   **Diego Maradona**   **Ryan Giggs**
(Dutch)   (Hungarian/Spanish)   (Argentine)   (Welsh)

Bobby Charlton   **Roberto Rivelino**
(English)   (Brazilian)

FANTASTIC FOOTBALL FACTS

REGIONAL RULERS

Club loyalty is a powerful force, but which players would you pick for a fantasy team to represent your region.

It's an almost impossible task, but that hasn't stopped us having a go with these suggestions...

LONDON XI

Peter Bonetti
(born Putney)

Stuart Pearce	**Bobby Moore**	**Tony Adams**	**Kenny Sansom**
(born Shepherd's Bush)	(born Barking)	(born Romford)	(born Camberwell)

Ray Wilkins	**David Beckham**	**Martin Peters**	**Glenn Hoddle**
(born Hillingdon)	(born Leytonstone)	(born Plaistow)	(born Hayes)

Jimmy Greaves
(born Poplar)

Ian Wright
(born Woolwich)

MIDLANDS XI

Peter Shilton
(born Leicester)

Phil Neal	**Billy Wright**	**Viv Anderson**	**Ray Wilson**
(born Irchester)	(born Ironbridge)	(born Nottingham)	(born Shirebrook)

Duncan Edwards	**Stanley Matthews**	**Adrian Heath**	**Garth Crooks**
(born Dudley)	(born Stoke)	(born Newcastle-under-Lyne)	(born Stoke)

Bob Latchford
(born Birmingham)

Gary Lineker
(born Leicester)

A FIST FULL OF FOOTBALLERS

GREATER MANCHESTER XI

Steven Bywater
(born Manchester)

Gary Neville
(born Bury)

Phil Neville
(born Bury)

Jimmy Armfield
(born Denton)

Wes Brown
(born Manchester)

Alan Ball
(born Farnworth)

David Platt
(born Oldham)

Paul Scholes
(born Salford)

Nicky Butt
(born Manchester)

Geoff Hurst
(born Ashton-under-Lyne)

Roger Hunt
(born Glazebury)

MERSEYSIDE XI

Tony Warner
(born Liverpool)

Brian Labone
(born Liverpool)

Tommy Smith
(born Liverpool)

Phil Thompson
(born Liverpool)

Jamie Carragher
(born Liverpool)

Jimmy Case
(born Liverpool)

Peter Reid
(born Liverpool)

Steve Coppell
(born Liverpool)

Steven Gerrard
(born Liverpool)

Robbie Fowler
(born Liverpool)

Dixie Dean
(born Birkenhead)

YORKSHIRE XI

Gordon Banks
(born Sheffield)

Trevor Cherry
(born Huddersfield)

Mick McCarthy
(born Barnsley)

John Scales
(born Harrogate)

Terry Cooper
(born Leeds)

David Batty
(born Bradford)

Stuart McCall
(born Leeds)

Paul Madeley
(born Leeds)

Kevin Davies
(born Sheffield)

Kevin Keegan
(born Armthorpe)

Alan Smith
(born Leeds)

FANTASTIC FOOTBALL FACTS

NORTH-EAST XI

Steve Simonsen
(born South Shields)

Jonathan Woodgate
(born Middlesbrough)

Jack Charlton
(born Ashington, Co. Durham)

Steve Bruce
(born Newcastle)

Norman Hunter
(born Eighton Banks)

Bobby Charlton
(born Ashington, Co. Durham)

Bryan Robson
(born Chester-le-Street, Co. Durham)

Chris Waddle
(born Gateshead)

Paul Gascoigne
(born Gateshead)

Peter Beardsley
(born Newcastle)

Alan Shearer
(born Gosforth)

GREATEST ENGLAND XIS

Everybody loves to argue about who would get into the best-ever England team.

Thanks to TheFA.com website, we bring you the verdicts of some of the greatest names ever to wear the Three Lions on their chest. . .

Alan Shearer

Peter Shilton
(1970–1990)

Phil Neal
(1976–83)

Bobby Moore
(1962–73)

Tony Adams
(1987–2001)

Stuart Pearce
(1987–1999)

David Beckham
(1996–)

Bryan Robson
(1980–91)

Paul Gascoigne
(1989–98)

Chris Waddle
(1985–92)

Bobby Charlton
(1958–70)

Gary Lineker
(1984–92)

Sir Tom Finney

Gordon Banks
(1963–72)

Jimmy Armfield (1959–66)	**Bobby Moore** (1962–73)	**Neil Franklin** (1947–50)	**Ray Wilson** (1960–68)
Stanley Matthews (1934–57)	**Duncan Edwards** (1955–57)	**David Beckham** (1996–)	**Bobby Charlton** (1958–70)

Jimmy Greaves
(1959–67)

Tommy Lawton
(1939–49)

John Barnes

Gordon Banks
(1963–72)

Phil Neal (1976–83)	**Bobby Moore** (1962–73)	**Duncan Edwards** (1955–57)	**Kenny Sansom** (1979–88)
Bobby Charlton (1958–70)	**Bryan Robson** (1980–91)	**Glenn Hoddle** (1979–88)	**Stanley Matthews** (1934–57)

Gary Lineker
(1984–92)

Nat Lofthouse
(1951–59)

Sir Geoff Hurst

Gordon Banks
(1963–72)

Alf Ramsey (1949–54)	**Bobby Moore** (1962–73)	**Tony Adams** (1987–2001)	**Ray Wilson** (1960–1968)
Duncan Edwards (1955–57)	**Bobby Charlton** (1958–70)	**Bryan Robson** (1980–91)	**Tom Finney** (1947–59)

Jimmy Greaves
(1959–67)

Alan Shearer
(1992–2000)

FANTASTIC FOOTBALL FACTS

Trevor Brooking

Peter Shilton
(1970–1990)

| **Duncan Edwards** | **Bobby Moore** | **Billy Wright** | **Kenny Sansom** |
| (1976–83) | (1962–73) | (1947–59) | (1979–88) |

| **David Beckham** | **Bobby Charlton** | **Bryan Robson** | **Tom Finney** |
| (1996–) | (1958–70) | (1980–91) | (1947–59) |

Kevin Keegan   **Gary Lineker**
(1972–82)   (1984–92)

Alan Ball

Gordon Banks
(1963–72)

| **Jimmy Armfield** | **Bobby Moore** | **Billy Wright** | **Ray Wilson** |
| (1959–66) | (1962–73) | (1947–59) | (1960–68) |

| **Stanley Matthews** | **Johnny Haynes** | **Duncan Edwards** | **Tom Finney** |
| (1934–57) | (1955–62) | (1955–57) | (1947–59) |

Jimmy Greaves   **Bobby Charlton**
(1959–67)   (1958–70)

Terry Butcher

Peter Shilton
(1970–1990)

George Cohen
(1964–68)

Bobby Moore
(1962–73)

Duncan Edwards
(1955–57)

Stuart Pearce
(1987–1999)

Stanley Matthews
(1934–57)

Bryan Robson
(1980–91)

Paul Gascoigne
(1989–98)

Tom Finney
(1947–59)

Geoff Hurst
(1965–72)

Michael Owen
(1998–)

Jimmy Armfield

Gordon Banks
(1963–72)

Roger Byrne
(1954–57)

Terry Butcher
(1980–90)

Bobby Moore
(1962–73)

**Cornelius (Neil)
Franklin**
(1947–50)

Duncan Edwards
(1955–57)

Bryan Robson
(1980–91)

Stanley Matthews
(1934–57)

Tom Finney
(1947–59)

Jimmy Greaves
(1959–67)

Alan Shearer
(1992–2000)

FANTASTIC FOOTBALL FACTS

Sir Bobby Robson

Gordon Banks
(1963–72)

Jimmy Armfield
(1959–66)

Bobby Moore
(1962–73)

Billy Wright
(1947–59)

Ray Wilson
(1960–68)

Stanley Matthews
(1934–57)

Johnny Haynes
(1955–62)

Tom Finney
(1947–59)

Bryan Robson
(1980–91)

Jimmy Greaves
(1959–67)

Bobby Charlton
(19584–70)

Stuart Pearce

Peter Shilton
(1970–1990)

George Cohen
(1964–68)

Bobby Moore
(1962–73)

Des Walker
(1989–93)

Kenny Sansom
(1979–88)

Bobby Charlton
(1958–70)

Paul Gascoigne
(1989–98)

Bryan Robson
(1980–91)

Stanley Matthews
(1934–57)

Gary Lineker
(1984–92)

Alan Shearer
(1992–2000)

CAP THAT

Who is the greatest-ever England striker? Which central defenders deserve to be selected for Scotland's ultimate side?

Arguments will always rage, but here is the definitive team for each of the Home Nations based on most caps won by players in each position.

England XI

Peter Shilton
(1970–1990) 125 caps

Bobby Moore	**Billy Wright**	**Kenny Sansom**	**Stuart Pearce**
(1962–73) 108 caps	(1947–59) 105 caps	(1979–88) 86 caps	(1987–99) 78 caps

Bryan Robson	**Ray Wilkins**	**John Barnes**	**Tom Finney**
(1980–91) 90 caps	(1976–86) 84 caps	(1983–95) 78 caps	(1946–58) 76 caps

Bobby Charlton   **Gary Lineker**
(1958–70) 106 caps   (1984–92) 80 caps

Scotland XI

Jim Leighton
(1982–98) 91 caps

Tom Boyd	**Alex McLeish**	**Willie Miller**	**Danny McGrain**
(1990–2001) 72 caps	(1980–93) 77 caps	(1975–89) 65 caps	(1973–82) 62 caps

Paul McStay	**Kenny Dalglish**	**John Collins**	**Gary McAllister**
(1983–97) 76 caps	(1971–86) 102 caps	(1988–99) 58 caps	(1990–99) 57 caps

Ally McCoist   **Denis Law**
(1985–98) 61 caps   (1958–74) 55 caps

FANTASTIC FOOTBALL FACTS

Wales XI

Neville Southall
(1982–98) 92 caps

Joey Jones	**Andy Melville**	**Kevin Ratcliffe**	**David Phillips**
(1976–86) 72 caps	(1989–2004) 63 caps	(1981–93) 59 caps	(1984–98) 62 caps
Peter Nicholas	**Brian Flynn**	**Gary Speed**	**Mark Hughes**
(1979–92) 73 caps	(1975–84) 66 caps	(1990–2004) 80 caps	(1984–99) 72 caps

Dean Saunders
(1986–2001) 75 caps

Ian Rush
(1980–96) 73 caps

Northern Ireland XI

Pat Jennings
(1964–86) 119 caps

Mal Donaghy	**Jimmy Nicholl**	**Terry Neill**	**Nigel Worthington**
(1980–94) 91 caps	(1976–86) 73 caps	(1961–73) 59 caps	(1984–77) 66 caps
Martin O'Neill	**Sammy McIlroy**	**David McCreery**	**Billy Bingham**
(1972–85) 64 caps	(1972–87) 88 caps	(1976–90) 67 caps	(1951–64) 56 caps

Gerry Armstrong
(1977–86) 63 caps

Iain Dowie
(1990–2000) 59 caps

BEST-EVER CLUB XIS
Comparing players from different eras may be virtually impossible, but that doesn't stop fans arguing every week down the pub who they would pick in their club's best-ever side.

And to spice up those debates even more, here are our personal selections for Arsenal, Liverpool, Manchester United, Chelsea and Newcastle United's greatest ever players:

Gunning for Glory XI – Arsenal
David Seaman

Lee Dixon   Tony Adams   Sol Campbell   Pat Rice

George Armstrong   Patrick Vieira   Liam Brady   Robert Pieres

Thierry Henry   Cliff Bastin

Manager – Arsene Wenger

Mersey Magic XI – Liverpool
Bruce Grobbelaar

Phil Neal   Alan Hansen   Tommy Smith   Emlyn Hughes

Kenny Dalglish   Graeme Souness   Steven Gerrard   John Barnes

Ian Rush   Michael Owen

Manager – Bill Shankly

FANTASTIC FOOTBALL FACTS

True Blue XI – Chelsea

Peter Bonetti

Ron Harris   John Terry   William Gallas   Dave Webb

Charlie Cooke   Dennis Wise   Roberto di Matteo   Gianfranco Zola

Peter Osgood   Bobby Tambling

Manager – Ruud Gullit

Red Devils XI – Manchester United

Peter Schmeichel

Duncan Edwards   Steve Bruce   Jaap Stam   Denis Irwin

Ryan Giggs   Bobby Charlton   Roy Keane   George Best

Denis Law   Ruud van Nistelrooy

Manager – Alex Ferguson

On the Toon XI – Newcastle United

Willie McFaul

Billy McCracken   Frank Brennan   Bobby Moncur   Bobby Cowell

Terry McDermott   Paul Gascoigne   Chris Waddle   Peter Beardsley

Alan Shearer   Jackie Milburn

Manager – Bobby Robson

THEY SAID WHAT?

Footballers are paid for playing football, but talking a good game is also part of the job these days. Sometimes, only a footballer can express himself with such clarity as these examples show. You know it makes sense.

'Alex Ferguson is the best manager I've ever had at this level. Well, he's the only manager I've actually had at this level. But he's the best manager I've ever had.' – *David Beckham*

'If you don't believe you can win, there is no point in getting out of bed at the end of the day.' – *Neville Southall*

'We lost because we didn't win.' – *Ronaldo*

'I've had 14 bookings this season – 8 of which were my fault, but 7 of which were disputable.' – *Paul Gascoigne*

'I've never wanted to leave. I'm here for the rest of my life, and hopefully after that as well.' – *Alan Shearer*

'I'd like to play for an Italian club, like Barcelona.' – *Mark Draper*

'You've got to believe that you're going to win, and I believe we'll win the World Cup until the final whistle blows and we're knocked out.' – *Peter Shilton*

'I faxed a transfer request to the club at the beginning of the week, but let me state that I don't want to leave Leicester.' – *Stan Collymore*

FANTASTIC FOOTBALL FACTS

'I was watching the Blackburn game on TV on Sunday when it flashed on the screen that George (Ndah) had scored in the first minute at Birmingham. My first reaction was to ring him up. Then I remembered he was out there playing.' – *Ade Akinbiyi*

'Without being too harsh on David Beckham, he cost us the match.' – *Ian Wright*

'I'm as happy as I can be – but I have been happier.' – *Ugo Ehiogu*

'Leeds is a great club and it's been my home for years, even though I live in Middlesbrough.' – *Jonathan Woodgate*

'I can see the carrot at the end of the tunnel.' – *Stuart Pearce*

'I took a whack on my left ankle, but something told me it was my right.' – *Lee Hendrie.*

'I couldn't settle in Italy – it was like living in a foreign country.' – *Ian Rush*

'If you're 0–0 down, there's no one better to get you back on terms than Ian Wright.' – *Robbie Earle*

'Germany are a very difficult team to play . . . they had 11 internationals out there today.' – *Steve Lomas*

'I always used to put my right boot on first, and then obviously my right sock.' – *Barry Venison*

'The Brazilians were South American, and the Ukrainians will be more European.' – *Phil Neville*

'The opening ceremony was good, although I missed it.' – *Graeme Le Saux*

'I'd rather play in front of a full house than an empty crowd.' – *Johnny Giles*

'Sometimes in football you have to score goals.' – *Thierry Henry*

'I was surprised, but I always say nothing surprises me in football.' – *Les Ferdinand*

'There's no in-between – you're either good or bad. We were in between.' – *Gary Lineker*

'Winning doesn't really matter as long as you win.' – *Vinnie Jones*

SOCCER SLANG

Ever thought that footballers and pundits speak a language all of their own?

Here we explain some of the more common terms in the footballers lexicon.

'At the end of the day. . .' – Used to sum a game up, or the time when footballers gear up for a big night on the town.

'As sick as a parrot' – Very upset, although usually used in conjunction with a series of expletives.

'A carbon copy of the first. . .' – Similar to something that has happened already.

'It's a game of two halves' – One of the favoured clichés of the modern game used to describe a game being turned on its head. Footballers have also been known to enjoy two halves, sometimes more, in the bar afterwards.

'He's stuck it in the onion bag' – Scored a goal. Does not have to occur in France.

'Put it in the mixer' – When a winger crosses the ball into the penalty area. Unless used by Norwich director Delia Smith when baking a cake.

FANTASTIC FOOTBALL FACTS

'Early doors' – Not a reference to Jim Morrison's band, but a term used to signify the period at the start of a game.

'Early bath' – What a player takes when he has been sent off. Well used when talking about Dennis Wise, Paul Ince and Roy Keane.

'Take a gamble', 'Have a go', 'Have a dig' – All used to describe a player who has a speculative shot on goal or makes a speculative run into the penalty area. Often shouted at Jamie Carragher without reward.

'Nuts' – A nutmeg. Where a player kicks the ball through the legs of another and collects it on the other side.

And introducing a special category which has become known as Ronglish. . .

'Lollipops' – A new entry to the fabulous football dictionary, thanks to Ron Atkinson. When a player steps over the ball to confuse the defender.

'Spotters' badge' – Atkinson created this term to signify that a player had seen a team-mate in a superb position and picked him out with a quality pass.

'Wide Awake Club' – Timmy Mallett will be proud that Big Ron took his famous kids TV show and fashioned a term to highlight when a player was really alert.

'Hollywood Ball' – Atkinson again as he plunders the glamorous world of the movies to describe a long-range pass that deserves a starring role.

'Full gun' – Why use the word powerful or venomous or stinging to describe a shot when you can instead say that Paul Scholes has given it 'the full gun' from the edge of the box?

CELEBRITY FANS

The popularity of football has gone through the roof in the past ten years with pop stars, esteemed authors and even Hollywood A-list movie legends declaring their allegiance to various clubs. But who exactly are the celebs cheering on and why?

Holly Valance (Southampton) – The former *Neighbours* actress turned singer is a Saints fan courtesy of her mum Rachel who was born in Southampton before she emigrated to Australia.

Patrick Stewart (Huddersfield Town) – Star Trek's captain Jean-Luc Picard regularly used to boldly go to Leeds Road – Town's former home – having been born and raised in nearby Mirfield. He was also appointed Chancellor of Huddersfield University in 2004.

Halle Berry (Everton) – The Bond girl is another to have inherited her allegiance via her mother. Halle's mum was born and raised in Liverpool and was a lifelong Toffees fan.

Hugh Grant (Fulham) – Grant, star of *Four Weddings and a Funeral*, grew up in nearby Chiswick and once revealed: 'I'd hate to be ever again the man who cleaned the seats at Fulham Football Club, which is a job I once had.'

Cameron Diaz (Brentford) – Follows the mighty Bees from Hollywood via friend and restaurateur Dan Tana – former chairman at Griffin Park.

Robert Duvall (Boca Juniors) – The respected Hollywood actor was converted to soccer by his Argentinian girlfriend and even went on to make a football movie called 'The Cup' set in Scotland featuring Ally McCoist and Alex Ferguson.

Arnold Schwarzenneger (Sturm Graz) – The Governor of California was born in the Austrian city of Graz and the club's stadium is actually named after the muscle man.

FANTASTIC FOOTBALL FACTS

Michael Grade (Charlton Athletic) – The BBC chairman only agreed to take up his post with Auntie on the understanding he could continue as a director at his beloved Charlton. 'I told them I was prepared to give up Camelot, but that giving up Charlton was a deal breaker,' he revealed.

Salman Rushdie (Tottenham) – The *Satanic Verses* author was forced into exile in 1989 after Ayatollah Khomeini – adamant the book was anti-Muslim – issued a fatwa leading to Iranian militants offering $2.5m for his murder. Perhaps worse still, Rushdie has supported Spurs all his life and even wrote an essay called 'The People's Game' about the club.

CELEBRITY FOOTBALLERS

Many people dream of being professional footballers, but unfortunately things do not always turn out as planned. Here we list some men who had to look for another route to fame after failing to make it in the world's greatest game.

Rod Stewart

He currently spends his time playing his smash hit records in front of thousands of adoring fans and leggy beauty Penny Lancaster. But things could have turned out very differently for Rod had he not been turned away by Brentford following an apprenticeship spell with the Bees in the early 1960s.

Nicky Byrne

Byrne spent his youth with dreams of becoming a professional footballer as a trainee goalkeeper with Leeds United. Things didn't work out for the teenage heart-throb though and he turned his attention to the music scene and continues to please millions of kids as part of world-famous boy band Westlife.

Angus Deayton
Before setting out as a television presenter Deayton had high hopes of becoming a professional footballer. He had trials with Crystal Palace, but things didn't work out and he moved into television work.

Gordon Ramsey
He is now known for his cooking skills as one of Britain's top chefs, but Ramsey could have been running out in front of 50,000 mad Glasgow Rangers fans if his football career had not turned pear-shaped.

Bradley Walsh
Walsh is a self-labelled funny man, who spent his early years as a professional at Brentford. Two years and several injuries later he was back on a factory production line only to change careers again – this time moving into the glamorous world of television.

Harvey
The So Solid Crew member spent his youth with Chelsea before moving into the non-League scene once his music career kicked into gear. He more recently played for AFC Wimbledon before moving to Ryman League side Lewes.

Julio Iglesias
The Spanish crooner was a young keeper who had a trial with the mighty Real Madrid before finding an easier way to make money and meet girls.

The Pope
The chief Roman Catholic, real name Karol Wojtyla, was a goal-keeper in his youth and now supports Liverpool where his fave player, according to fellow Polish shot-stopper Jerzy Dudek, is

FANTASTIC FOOTBALL FACTS

Jerzy Dudek. Quoting from the Liverpool website, via the BBC website, Dudek said: 'I spoke to a couple of guys who are very close to the Pope and they told me that he is always watching our games and that he is always thinking of me when Liverpool play.'

Luciano Pavarotti
Football was his first love when the rotund opera singer was a touch more svelte and he was a star child footballing performer for Modena, his local town's team.

RELATIVE SUCCESS
For many a schoolboy the prospect of playing top-flight football is all but a dream. Others aspire to follow in their father's footsteps or work in the family business. The select few get to do both and a handful of father–son combinations have even achieved an even more remarkable feat – playing for England.

Eastham
The first father and son to have played for England – the George Easthams, senior and junior, made history in 1963 when George junior won the first of his 19 international caps.

His father George 'Diddler' Eastham was a Bolton Wanderers and Brentford player in the 30s, who made his England appearance in 1935.

Eastham junior played for Arsenal, Newcastle and Stoke in a career spanning three decades. A deft and creative inside-forward with the ability to provide a defence-splitting pass, George grabbed a League Cup-winning goal in 1972.

Eastham was also victorious in the High Court, where he historically challenged the 'retain and transfer' system that had prevented his move from Newcastle to Arsenal. George Eastham junior was awarded the OBE in 1973.

Clough

Outspoken former manager Brian Clough, who led Derby to the top of the league in 1972 and Nottingham Forest to both league and European Cup success in 1979 and 1980, earned himself two England caps in 1959. Clough's professional playing career had begun at Middlesbrough in 1955, where he scored 197 goals in 213 league games. After earning his caps against Wales and Sweden, Clough senior moved to Sunderland where he bagged another 54 goals in only 61 games.

Nigel Clough began his playing career in 1984 under the management of father Brian at Nottingham Forest. After netting over 100 goals in 311 appearances, Nigel joined Liverpool and then Man City before retiring injured. During his career Nigel won 14 full England caps to add to the family collection.

Lampard

Another father with a brace of England caps is Frank Lampard senior, West Ham's legendary full-back of the 70s and early 80s. Lampard clocked-up nearly 550 appearances for the Hammers after signing as an apprentice. After retiring as a player he eventually joined their coaching staff, together with brother-in-law Harry Redknapp.

Namesake son Frank Lampard followed in his father's footsteps, joining West Ham as a trainee in the early 90s. But both father and son departed from West Ham in 2001 as Frank junior secured an £11m move to Chelsea. After successful seasons at Stamford Bridge, Lampard pushed himself into the international frame and became a key player in the side ahead of Euro 2004.

Redknapp

Harry Redknapp's managerial career began at AFC Bournemouth, before his return to West Ham, where he spent eight seasons as a player. An attacking midfielder in his playing days, Redknapp also won youth honours for his country.

FANTASTIC FOOTBALL FACTS

Also at Bournemouth as an apprentice was Harry's son – Liverpool, Tottenham and England star Jamie Redknapp. Before injury plagued his last few seasons Jamie had done more than enough to escape the shadow of his father, with inspirational performances for both Liverpool and England in Euro 1996. Redknapp picked up 19 caps and 3 goals with the England Under–21 side, and a further 17 full appearances and a goal with the senior squad.

Charlton

The Northumberland-born Charlton brothers remain two of the best-recognised and most successful figures in the game. The first brothers ever to pull on their national team shirt, both went on to collect a World Cup-winners' medal in 1966. While brother Bobby joined Manchester United, Jack spent his entire playing career at Leeds Utd, scoring 96 goals in 773 appearances, plus 35 appearances for England. As a manager 'Big Jack' led Middlesbrough into Division 1 and had spells at both Sheffield Wednesday and Newcastle before moving into international management. As the first non-Irishman to hold the post of Republic of Ireland manager, his appointment was initially a controversial one, but that was soon forgotten after the Republic qualified for both the 1990 and 1994 World Cup Finals, famously defeating Italy in 1994.

In the late 1960s brother Bobby was dubbed 'the most famous living Englishman' by pundit Jimmy Hill. The Football Writers' Player of the Year in 1967, Charlton had survived the 1958 Munich air disaster that killed 21 and decimated Sir Matt Busby's Manchester United 'babes'. Bobby Charlton went on to secure three League Division 1 titles, one FA Cup, a European Cup, 106 international caps and 49 goals – and of course that elusive FIFA World Cup-winners' medal.

Wallace

Danny Wallace was one of Southampton's most exciting players, making more than 300 appearances for the club between 1980 and

156

1989 after debuting at the age of 16 – the Saints' youngest-ever first-team player.

Tragically, after winning the FA Cup and European Cup-Winners' Cup under Alex Ferguson, Wallace's £1.2m transfer to Manchester United in 1989 was marred by ever-worsening injuries and in 1996 he was forced to retire after being diagnosed with MS.

However, in the interim, Wallace had managed to score in his first and only appearance in an England shirt against Egypt in 1986, and made history once again.

In 1988 Danny and his brothers, Rod and Ray, played alongside each other in a First Division match for the Saints.

Summerbee

Three generations of the Summerbee family have had distinguished playing careers. Brothers Gordon and George played at Aldershot Town, before George moved on to Preston North End.

George's famous son is former Manchester City star Mike Summerbee, whose son Nicky also had spells at the club before joining Bradford City in 2003.

Other top-flight footballing brothers include Phil and Gary Neville, of Manchester United and England.

Cousins Les Ferdinand and Rio, together with his brother Anton, all played for West Ham.

FUNNY OLD JOB

Every football fan in the world lives in the hope that he will one day be 'discovered' and go on to play for his country. Here are a few of the men who successfully 'gave up the day job'. . .

David Wetherall – Chemistry student

Always a surprise to see footballers with more than an O level or two, David Wetherall went a few steps further and got a degree. As a student he almost accepted a job in the lab before becoming a footballer.

Gilberto Silva – Sweet-factory worker, quarry worker and furniture manufacturer.

As the only male child in a large family, Gilberto, gave up a promising football career to support his family when his father retired. After three years of dead-end jobs he was persuaded to give football another go by his friends.

Chris Waddle – Sausage stuffer

As a youngster handling sausages for a living, few would have thought that Waddle would play as a professional footballer for 20 years, grow a mullet, and miss a penalty in the World Cup semi-final ... but he did.

Dean Windass – Bricklayer

After an unsuccessful YTS placement with Hull City, Deano combined working as a brickie with playing up front for his local side, before being signed by the Tigers.

Barry Hayles – Carpenter

The Lambeth-born Fulham striker plied his trade as a 'chippie' before hitting the big time and going on to represent Jamaica at international level.

Steve Jones – Soap-factory worker

Despite never really making his name on the big stage, Jones had been working in a soap factory before signing for West Ham. A journalist's dream, 'I'm forever blowing bubbles ...'

Les Ferdinand – Delivery driver, van steam cleaner, plasterer's mate.

'Sir' Les had a succession of manual jobs while playing non-League football. Once he signed as a pro he went on to win the PFA Player of the Year award and scored the Premier League's 10,000th goal.

Chris Armstrong – Bus cleaner

As a youngster in North Wales the would-be striker spent his time cleaning buses. When he went to Tottenham he had another unenviable task: trying to fill Jürgen Klinsmann's boots.

Bob Wilson – PE teacher

Having been told by his father to turn down an apprenticeship with Manchester United, Bob Primrose Wilson trained to be a PE teacher at Loughborough before joining Arsenal as an amateur in the early 1960s. He still taught part-time for five years in North London before signing professional terms with the Gunners.

HOW DID THEY MANAGE THAT?

Every manager would love to be in charge of Manchester United or Real Madrid, but unfortunately the vast majority have to find their employment elsewhere.

And some coaches end up at completely the opposite end of the spectrum with the weirdest and most wonderful managerial jobs.

Howard Wilkinson

The one-time temporary England manager swapped Sheffield for Shanghai in March 2004.

The Yorkshireman claimed Shanghai Shenua were the 'Manchester United of China' and explained: 'I spoke to Arsene Wenger and he said that it was a very beneficial experience when he went to Japan. He came back having learned from a different culture, which has made him a better manager.

'My job is to come up with a three- to five-year plan to move this club forward.'

However, the plan was shorter than expected as Wilkinson returned to England just two months later due to personal reasons.

Mick Wadsworth
When Wadsworth was sacked as manager of Third Division Huddersfield Town you would have got very long odds on him leading an international side into the 2004 African Nations Cup just two seasons later.

But that's exactly what happened as the man who had also failed to set the football world alight in charge of Carlisle and Colchester was suddenly appointed manager of Congo.

However, Congo lost all three games in the African Nations Cup and Wadsworth fumed: 'The whole thing was a disaster from minute one. It was really chatotic and bizarre at times.

'I had no control whatsoever of where we went for the training camps and I had no control of the selection of players.'

Philippe Troussier
The 'white witch doctor' made his name with Nigeria when he took them to the 1998 World Cup – but was sacked before they actually got to France – before spells with South Africa, Burkina Faso and Japan. Now busy poaching Brazilians for the Qatar national side.

Joe Kinnear
The former Crazy Gang manager and current Nottingham Forest boss had a brief stint as head coach of Nepal in 1981.

Arsène Wenger
Before he made his name at Arsenal he had already pulled up trees in Japan where he took bottom-three side Nagoya Grampus-Eight to second place in the J-League, winning a Super Cup along the way.

But his tenure in Japan didn't start as well as he'd hoped, and he was quoted as saying after a run of bad results: 'I thought they would sack me, but instead they got rid of my translator!'

Steve Perryman
Perryman managed Norwegian side Start before pairing up with his old Spurs team-mate Ossie Ardiles at Shimizu S-Pulse in Japan. He won the Japan League Cup in his first season in charge, before clinching the league championship three years later. After hitting the heights in Japan he left in 2000 to help Exeter City in their bid to claw their way out of the Conference. Unfortunately, they were relegated at the end of the 2002–3 season.

Guus Hiddink
From PSV to Real Madrid to ... Korea. Hiddink's move from the playground of football in Europe to manage a team he couldn't even understand certainly raised eyebrows – until he led them to the semi-finals of the World Cup.

FAMOUS REJECTS
We all know it's not just ability that takes players to the top. In every successful team there is a Martin Keown, as well as a Thierry Henry.

It's determination like his that keeps kids going when told as a schoolboy that 'you're not good enough'. Here we look at some of those players who went on to prove the doubters wrong ...

1. David Platt – Manchester United 1985
Five years before 'that goal' against Belgium in the 1990 World Cup Finals, a young David Platt was let go by Big Ron Atkinson. Platt went on to rack up more than £20m in transfer fees – well done Ron!

2. Robbie Savage – Manchester United 1994
The feisty Welsh midfielder was also released by the Red Devils, managed at that time by Sir Alex Ferguson. A solid, if unspectacular player, some would say Fergie got it right.

FANTASTIC FOOTBALL FACTS

3. David Seaman – Leeds United 1982
Twenty years before Ronaldinho left him down and out, a young David Seaman – moustache and all – was shown the door at Elland Road by Eddie Gray.

4. Lee Dixon – Burnley 1984
Arguably Arsenal's greatest-ever right back, winning four League titles, three FA cups, and more besides. Just think what he could have achieved at Burnley!

5. Matt Holland – West Ham United 1995
The Charlton midfielder failed to make the grade at West Ham, but was given a chance at Bournemouth, before making his name at Ipswich. While he was with the Tractor Boys remarkably he missed only one game in six years.

6. Kevin Nolan – Liverpool 1999
Nolan came through the youth team of his hometown club before being released and consequently snapped up by Bolton. Poignantly, he scored for the Trotters on his Anfield return.

7. Shaun Wright-Phillips – Nottingham Forest 1998
The adopted son of Arsenal legend Ian Wright was rejected by Forest for being too small. He has made a name for himself at Manchester City, forcing his way into the England squad and winning a nomination for PFA Young Player of the Year.

8. Andy Cole – Arsenal 1992
Despite being released by the Gunners at an early age, Cole went on to win five Premier League titles with Manchester United, playing a key role in their historic Treble in 1999.

9. Nigel Winterburn – Oxford United 1983, Birmingham City 1983
Part of Arsenal's fabled back four, the left back was rejected not once, but twice. Winterburn had the determination to fight on after such disappointment, a fighting spirit that was always apparent when he was playing.

10. Eric Cantona – Chelsea 1992
Chelsea manager Ian Porterfield was asked if he wanted to buy the mercurial Frenchman for £1m, but said no. The Gallic striker joined Leeds United and the rest is history.

ON THE SCREEN

Many footballers stand accused of play-acting when tackled and go to ground so quickly you would be forgiven for thinking there was a sniper in the crowd. The following cloggers turned thespians have tried to take it to another level.

Vinnie Jones
Jones has made the transition from pitch to screen seamlessly. Having got his big break in *Lock, Stock and Two Smoking Barrels*, the mild-mannered midfielder has since appeared in *Snatch*, *Mean Machine* and *Gone in 60 Seconds*.

Bobby Moore
As well as appearing in *Escape to Victory*, England and West Ham captain Moore was the face of British public houses in the 1960s. He appeared in TV adverts encouraging people to frequent their local boozer.

Eric Cantona
Having retired from football at a young age, Cantona could be seen in *Elizabeth* as a French courtier and numerous other French-backed film projects as well as being a regular in adverts for Nike products.

Scott Parker
Years before turning pro, Parker could be spotted in a McDonald's advert before the 1994 World Cup. Parker, then a gifted 14–year-old,

FANTASTIC FOOTBALL FACTS

was filmed doing a number of kick-ups and fancy tricks in his back garden.

Jeff Astle
The England striker bagged a regular spot on David Baddiel and Frank Skinner's Fantasy Football show where he would end the programme by crooning a classic song.

Robbie Keane and Graham Le Saux
Both players have made cameo appearances on the BBC sports agent sit-com, *Trevor's World of Sport*.

David Ginola
The highly coiffured Frenchman was the front man for a well-known brand of shampoo and appeared in a number of their adverts.

Pierluigi Collina
Collina has six times been voted the best referee on the planet and has cropped up in adverts and pop videos. He was even voted Italy's sexiest man when he appeared on the catwalk in Milan fashion week.

ANYTHING FOR MONEY

You'd think they earn enough cash on the pitch, but some players still accept big brown envelopes from companies desperate to associate themselves with football. Some of the adverts are amusing, some are cringeworthy, but all of them have grabbed the attention ...

Gareth Southgate

The England defender made fun of his penalty miss in the shoot-out against Germany in the semi-final of Euro '96 by appearing in an advert for Pizza Hut, where he starred alongside Chris Waddle and Stuart Pearce, who had missed their penalties against the Germans six years earlier.

Some fans still found it hard to swallow.

Kevin Keegan

Years after his playing career finished, Keegan's name still conjured images for a generation of the British public of a short man with a bubble perm splashing himself with Brut aftershave in the company of other bare-chested sports stars such as Henry Cooper. The great smell of Brut was the catchline.

Vinnie Jones

The former Wimbledon and Wales midfielder-turned-movie-star traded on his hardman image to make a series of ads for Bacardi Rum, which usually involved him looking mean and moody until he discovers the Latin Spirit. Hard to see Michael Owen doing the same.

Gary Lineker

Lineker's association with Walker's Crisps goes back a decade and the former England captain is probably better known through his ads and appearances on *Match of the Day* than for his time as the golden boy of English football during the late 80s and early 90s. He even had a flavour named after him – Salt'n'Lineker.

Bobby Moore
The World Cup-winning captain of England and West Ham starred in a 1960s advert for going down the pub that would cause outrage if today's breed of (mostly) teetotal players were to appear. Moore and his team-mate Martin Peters were filmed in their local, meeting their wives, playing darts and holding a pint of beer – imagine Posh and Becks doing that now!

Pat Jennings
The former Spurs and Northern Ireland keeper appeared in one of the most surreal adverts in football history, transformed into a giant oil filter for car repair company Unipart. Jennings, who was arguably the greatest keeper in the world at his peak in the mid-70s, was seen dressed as the car-part, diving around in a muddy goal-mouth – and looking more than slightly embarrassed.

Michael Owen
As befits his whiter-than-white image, Owen advertises washing powder, suggesting that even at the age of five he was hammering home goals by the dozen while his white shirt (with number 10 of course) hardly got a speck of mud – and if it did, Mum was there to wash it.

Ron Atkinson and Co.
Carling had one of the most memorable football ads when they mocked up a medieval scene with soldiers and serfs kicking around empty beer cans, overseen by Big Ron as the lord of the manor.

Brazil
Nike kick-started the trend for ads starring a whole host of top players in an unlikely setting, and one of the first to capture the public's

imagination was when the whole Brazil squad indulged in their repertoire of tricks, flicks and step-overs, while running through an airport, shortly before the 1998 World Cup. Needless to say airport security would not have been too pleased if any other team had tried it!

David Beckham

The England captain has appeared in plenty of ads, but none caused so much controversy as the time he mocked the weather and facilities at Manchester United soon after joining Real Madrid. In the Vodafone ad, Beckham takes a picture of the sunny sky above him in Spain and sends it as a picture message to the Neville brothers back in a wet and grey Manchester – Sir Alex Ferguson was far from amused.

ONLY IN THE MOVIES

With so many books written about football it is only right that, as art reflects life, we should have a host of movies about football. And, let's face it, even a film about Sheffield United has got to be better than sitting through *Titanic*!

Arsenal Stadium Mystery (1939) – The all-conquering 1938 Highbury squad help detective Leslie Banks investigate the death of an opposition player, killed during a 'friendly' match. Most of the Arsenal team, including manager George Allison, play themselves in this classic sporting film.

Kes (1969) – A gritty adaptation of *A Kestrel For A Knave* tells of the brutal upbringing and school days in the People's Republic of Yorkshire in the late 60s. Baldy wrestler Brian Glover will be forever remembered for his performance as the bullying PE teacher who lived out his Bobby Charlton penalty fantasy during one lesson. Classic stuff.

FANTASTIC FOOTBALL FACTS

Die Angst Des Tormannes Beim Elfmeter (The Goalkeeper's Fear of the Penalty / The Goalie's Anxiety at the Penalty Kick) (1971) – Wim Wenders' film shows that there is more to football than mindlessly chasing a pig's bladder around for 90 minutes. Goalkeeper Joseph Bloch (Brauss) inexplicably walks off the field mid-game and roams the streets of Berlin in a poor attempt to find himself. His bizarre change of behaviour results in the random murder of a cinema usher before heading for the countryside in an attempt to patch things up with his former lover.

The Likely Lads – James Bolam and Rodney Bewes spend the entire day trying to avoid the result of an important England game so that they can enjoy the highlights more – with hilarious results.

Yesterday's Hero (1979) – Ian McShane followed in the footsteps of his father, Manchester United winger Harry McShane, when he played a George Best-style maverick trying to make a comeback. Unfortunately this is not one of Jackie Collins's better efforts and is almost dire enough to put anyone off football.

Porridge (1979) – The film spin-off of the popular TV sit-com sees our hapless heroes, Ronnie Barker and Richard Beckinsale, unwillingly escape from prison during a football match. The Laurel and Hardy of HM Slade then try to break back into prison to avoid getting into trouble.

Gregory's Girl (1981) – John Gordon-Sinclair stars in this comedy as a gawky teenager smitten by Dee Hepburn, the school's top footballer.

Escape to Victory (1981) – Clearly a vintage year for football films. A host of Hollywood actors joining forces with stars such as Pele, Bobby Moore, Ossie Ardiles, Martin Peters and, er, John Wark, to escape from a German prisoner-of-war camp at half-time during a 'friendly' against the prison guards. The POWs were due to escape at half-time but were trailing 4–1 and decided to play the second half and teach the Germans a lesson. The game ended 4–4 with keeper Robert Hatch, played by Sylvester Stallone, saving a last-minute penalty.

The teams were:

ALLIES (Visitors)

1. Robert Hatch (USA) (Sylvester Stallone)
2. Michael Fileu (Bel) (Paul Van Himst)
3. Cptn John Colby (UK) (Michael Caine)
4. Pieter Van Beck (Hol) (Co Prins)
5. Doug Clure (UK) (Russell Osman)
6. Terry Brady (UK) (Bobby Moore)
7. Arthur Hayes (Sco) (John Wark)
8. Carlos Rey (Arg) (Ossie Ardiles)
9. Sid Harmor (UK) (Mike Summerbee)
10. Luis Fernandez (Bra) (Pele)
11. Erik Borge (Denmark) (Soren Lindsted)

subs
Paul Wolchek (Pol) (Kazimariez Deyna) on for No. 7
Gunnar Hilsson (Nor)(Hallvar Thoresen) on for No. 4

Scorers: Brady 44, Rey 52, Clure 76, Fernandez 88, (Clure had goal disallowed 84)

(Honourable mention for Tony Lewis (Ire) (Kevin O'Callaghan) who broke his arm before the match)

GERMANS (Home)

1. Schmidt (Laurie Sivell)
2. Kuntz
3. Reinhard

FANTASTIC FOOTBALL FACTS

4. Baumann (Werner Roth)
5. Kuntz
6. Kuntz
7. Becker
8. Kuntz
9. General Bronte
10. Schmidt (Robin Turner)
11. Albrech

Scorers: Albrech 14, 41, Bronte 25, Baumann (pen) 31, (Baumann missed pen 90)

Final score: Germany 4 Allies 4 (4–1)
Att: 50,000

ID (1994): A study of how undercover copper Reece Dinsdale gets drawn into the world of football hooliganism that surrounds a fictional football team who bear a passing resemblance to Millwall.

When Saturday Comes (1995) – Before he was in *Lord of the Rings*, Sean Bean starred as a womanising, hard-drinking factory worker who struggles against adversity to get a lucky break with Sheffield United. How lucky indeed!

Fever Pitch (1996) – An adaptation of Nick Hornby's novel about an obsessed Arsenal fan whose love for the Gunners jeopardises his relationship with his girlfriend.

The Match (1999) – This comedy pits Richard E Grant's la-di-da bistro outfit against Max Beesley's pub team in a Scottish amateur football derby where local pride is not all that is at stake – the winner gets to keep the loser's establishment.

Mike Bassett: England Manager (2001) – Ricky Tomlinson lifts himself from his armchair to take on the role of an unlikely boss of the England team.

Bend it Like Beckham (2002) – Parminder Nagra has the talent on the pitch but, being an Asian girl, not the support of her family. The show is stolen by Keira Knightley wearing football shorts.

Shaolin Soccer (2003) – A US-released comedy set in Hong Kong where a down-and-out former player inspires a squad of Kung Fu masters to form an invincible soccer team.

ON THE HEAD

So footballers are thick are they? Apparently not. Here are some players who do not fit the football stereotype and prove that some are not as dumb as they look.

Shaka Hislop
Anyone would have to be mad to be a goalkeeper, and top stopper Hislop is possibly just that after qualifying as a rocket scientist. The goalkeeper has a degree in Mechanical Engineering and used to work for NASA.

Iain Dowie
The Crystal Palace manager had a successful career as a top striker, but he may not have had the nous to score so many goals without his intense education. Dowie gained a degree in Aeronautical Engineering at Hatfield Polytechinc before going on to obtain a Masters in Mechanical Engineering.

Steve Coppell
Having always been considered too small to make it as a professional footballer as a youngster, Coppell turned his attention to expanding his mind by studying economics at Liverpool University. Soon Tranmere spotted his talents, however, and before long Coppell was established as a Manchester United legend after making over 300 appearances for the Red Devils.

FANTASTIC FOOTBALL FACTS

Tony Adams
The former England man was quick to give himself something new to think about after retiring from Arsenal in 2002. Adams signed up for a Sports Science degree at Brunel University, which he completed before taking on the job as boss of Wycombe Wanderers.

Brian McClair
The former Manchester United striker studied for a Maths degree at university while starting his career at Motherwell.
The qualification came in handy as Brian had no trouble keeping tally of his goals as he hit the net.

David Wetherall
Wetherall studied for a Chemistry degree and represented Great Britain in the World Student Games of 1991. However, Wetherall turned his back on the science labs later in the year to join Leeds United as a professional.

Barry Horne
Like Wetherall, former Everton man Horne dismissed the 'dumb footballer' stereotype by gaining a degree in Chemistry.

Steve Palmer
The former Hornet and QPR boy is one of the game's few players to have the honour of being an Oxbridge graduate. Palmer gained an MSc in Computing.

Socrates
The Brazilian maestro stayed concentrated off the field to become a qualified paediatrician.

THE RICH LIST

Times are a-changing and the people's game has become a big business. Many clubs still run at a loss, though. This is a list of the 20 biggest clubs in Europe according to turnover. If nothing else, it really does prove that money does not usually buy success.

1. Manchester United £167.38m
2. Juventus £145.34m
3. AC Milan £133.27m
4. Real Madrid £128.2m
5. Bayern Munich £108.3m
6. Internazionale Milan £108.1m
7. Arsenal £100.6m
8. Liverpool £100.4m
9. Newcastle United £93.3m
10. Chelsea £89.9m
11. AS Roma £89.09m
12. Borussia Dortmund £83.4m
13. Barcelona £82.9m
14. Schalke 04 £79.7m
15. Tottenham Hotspur £64.3m
16. Leeds United £61.8m
17. SS Lazio £59.7m
18. Celtic £58.4m
19. Olympique Lyonnais £56.7m
20. Valencia £54.1m

*Figures from 2002–03 season
(Source Deloitte & Touche

RICHEST FOOTBALLERS

We all know that the world's best footballers are far from struggling on the financial front, but just how much cash do they really make?

FANTASTIC FOOTBALL FACTS

Each week some of the most talented players on the planet stroll up to the cash point to check they can afford to pay their bills ... and judging by these figures it's not too much of a problem.

FOOTBALL'S TOP SALARY EARNERS (PER WEEK)

DAVID BECKHAM (Real Madrid) £120,000

ROY KEANE (Manchester United) £94,000

RONALDO (Real Madrid) £90,000

ZINEDINE ZIDANE (Real Madrid) £90,000

RAUL (Real Madrid) £90,000

RIO FERDINAND (Manchester United) £72,000

SOL CAMPBELL (Arsenal) £72,000

MICHAEL OWEN (Liverpool) £68,000

ALESSANDRO DEL PIERO (Juventus) £68,000

CHRISTIAN VIERI (Inter Milan) £67,000

HIDETOSHI NAKATA (Parma) £61,000

A successful career often leads to sponsorship deals as well as added bonuses from club bosses. And as the wealth builds up Britain's top stars are left staring at a healthy bank balance.

WEALTHIEST BRITISH FOOTBALLERS

DAVID BECKHAM (joint wealth with wife Victoria) £65m

ROBBIE FOWLER £25m

MICHAEL OWEN £25m

SOL CAMPBELL £20m

RYAN GIGGS £17m

RIO FERDINAND £14m

JUAN VERON £14m

THIERRY HENRY £12m

EMILE HESKEY £9m

RUUD VAN NISTELROOY £9m

PATRICK VIEIRA £8m

WHAT A SAVE

Strikers normally grab all the glory with the all-important goals that win matches. But sometimes it's the man at the other end of the pitch that proves to be the hero. Here are the goalkeepers who quite rightly grabbed their moment in the spotlight ...

Gordon Banks – England v Brazil, 1970 World Cup
Probably the most famous save in the history of football. Banks produced a full-length dive across goal to keep out a powerful header from Brazil legend Pele.

Jim Montgomery – Sunderland v Leeds, 1973 FA Cup final
Underdogs Sunderland sprang a shock with a 1–0 win over Leeds thanks to Montgomery's heroics. His best save came when he kept out Trevor Cherry's header and twisted up from the turf to turn away Peter Lorimer's follow-up.

Bruce Grobbelaar – Liverpool v Everton, 1986 FA Cup final
Liverpool were trailing 1–0 to Merseyside rivals Everton when Grobbelaar sprung backwards to tip a goalbound Graeme Sharp header over the crossbar. Inspired by their keeper's save, the Anfield side then surged back to win 3–1.

Rene Higuita – Colombia v England, 1995 international friendly
Eccentric Colombian Higuita stunned Wembley with his astonishing airborne back-flick to clear the ball away after a long shot from England's Jamie Redknapp. It immediately became known as the

Scorpion, although the effort would not have counted anyway because of an offside flag.

Peter Schmeichel – Manchester United v Rapid Vienna, 1996 Champions League

Man Utd legend Schmeichel leaped across goal and managed to palm Rene Wagner's close-range header over the bar when it seemed the Austrian could not miss.

David Seaman – Arsenal v Sheffield United, 2003 FA Cup semi-final

Seaman kept Arsenal's bid for a double Double on course with one of the greatest saves of all time in their FA Cup semi-final win over Sheffield United. The Gunners were leading 1–0 when the England international flung himself to his right to keep out Paul Peschisolido's point-blank header with just six minutes left.

ALL OUT

They say they just love the game, but sometimes players threaten to stop the match and take their ball home with them.

Strike action has reared its ugly head a few times down the years in England, but so far the threats have always been averted. Next time, though'...

1909: The first threatened strike came a year after the players' union was formed and followed the FA's decision to withdraw recognition, fearing it was getting too strong. Some players resisted for 14 weeks without pay. Then the FA and union agreed to recognise each other and, as part of the deal, players received the wages they had forfeited. The union became the PFA in 1958.

1947: With football getting back on its feet after the Second World War, the players' union wanted a minimum wage level fixed for all full-time professionals. The issue went to an arbitration tribunal which awarded a minimum of £7 during the season and £5 in the summer for all those over 20.

1961: PFA leader Jimmy Hill threatened a strike if the £20 a week maximum wage was not abolished and warned the England squad would join it. The Football League and Ministry of Labour relented and the players' victory was confirmed when the High Court ruled in favour of George Eastham's wish to join Arsenal from Newcastle United.

1992: Amid wrangling over the introduction of the Premier League, players declared they would consider a strike if they did not get a big enough say in how the game was run. The decision to go ahead with the 'new' league was taken by the FA Council on 20 February, but arguments dragged on until the end of April when the PFA won a 50 per cent increase to £1.5m in the share of the money it received from television.

2001: The PFA served notice of a strike insisting that the amount of TV money from the Premier League and Football League was not enough. Action was called off when a new £52.5m, three-year offer was accepted.

BABY-FACED BOSSES

They say there is no substitute for experience, but that wasn't an option for the following managers who were thrown into the deep end at a young age. They might have been fresh-faced, but they soon had to toughen up after taking over these Premiership clubs ...

Attilio Lombardo (Crystal Palace, March 1998) aged 32 years 2 months
The Italian took on the role of player-manager when Steve Coppell left Selhurst Park. He was in charge for just six weeks, however, before Terry Venables arrived in the summer.

FANTASTIC FOOTBALL FACTS

Chris Coleman (Fulham, April 2003) aged 32 years 10 months
The former Welsh international had only just hung up his boots after
a serious car crash when Jean Tigana left Fulham. Coleman, who
had already started coaching at the west London club, was then pro-
moted to first-team manager, a position he retains after a satisfac-
tory 2003–04 season.

Gianluca Vialli (Chelsea, February 1998) aged 33 years 7 months
Vialli was already a crowd favourite as a player at Stamford Bridge
before adding the managerial role to his duties when Ruud Gullit
was sacked. The Italian was an immediate success and won the
European Cup-Winners' Cup, FA Cup and League Cup before being
sacked himself in 2000.

Ruud Gullit (Chelsea, May 1996) aged 33 years 8 months
The Dutch legend became player-manager when Glenn Hoddle left
to take over the England team. Gullit was an instant hit and won the
FA Cup – Chelsea's first trophy in 26 years – before being sacked in
1998.

Stuart Pearce (Nottm Forest, December 1996) aged 34 years 8 months
The Forest defender stepped into the breach when Frank Clark was
sacked with the club struggling at the bottom of the Premiership.
However, while contemplating his first team selection Pearce failed
to select a goalkeeper until his wife Liz pointed out his mistake and
it was no real surprise when he stepped down after five months.

Paul Jewell (Bradford City, May 1999) aged 34 years 8 months
Jewell had been reserve manager and first-team coach at Bradford
before replacing Chris Kamara. He took the Bantams into the top
flight for the first time in their history, performed heroics to keep
them in the Premiership and then handed in his resignation to join
Sheffield Wednesday.

Paul Goddard (Ipswich, December 1994) aged 35 years 2 months
Goddard was in temporary charge at Portman Road for just three games between the spells of John Lyall and George Burley. His record read two draws and one defeat.

Glenn Hoddle (Chelsea, June 1993) aged 35 years 8 months
The former England midfielder had already served his apprentice-ship in the lower leagues as manager of Swindon when Chelsea offered him the top job. He did not win any trophies at Stamford Bridge but is credited with beginning the revolution which lead to success for Ruud Gullit and Gianluca Vialli.

Peter Reid (Manchester City, May 1992) aged 35 years 10 months
Reid was well known as a no-nonsense midfield hardman and he has transferred that into management, starting with his three-year spell at Manchester City. He steered the club to fifth, fifth and ninth in the Premiership, but was sacked at the start of his fourth season in charge.

John Deehan (Norwich, January 1994) aged 36 years 5 months
Deehan was a hero at Carrow Road as a star striker, but his 18 months in charge of the Canaries proved disastrous. He stepped up from assistant manager when Mike Walker joined Everton, but Norwich plummeted down the table and Deehan resigned before they were eventually relegated in 1995.

DEATH THREATS
Fans usually adore their favourite players, put their posters on their walls and sing their name loud and proud in the stadium.

However, sometimes a bad performance or costly mistake can cause the supporters to turn against their former heroes and make life unbearable for them.

FANTASTIC FOOTBALL FACTS

Andres Escobar (June 1994) – Colombian Escobar was killed following an argument with a fan outside a bar in Bogota. He had just returned from the World Cup where his own goal in Colombia's World Cup defeat against the USA had cost his side their place in the competition.

David Beckham (July 1998) – Beckham was targeted after his sending-off in the World Cup against Argentina. He was sent death threats and an effigy of the Manchester United star was hung from an East London pub.

Michael Duberry (March 2001) – Leeds defender Duberry was sent hate mail and threats from his own club's fans after appearing in court to give evidence against team-mates Jonathan Woodgate and Lee Bowyer.

Neil Lennon (August 2002) – Lennon quit international football after receiving death threats which forced him to withdraw from a Northern Ireland friendly against Cyprus in Belfast. The Catholic player had angered Protestant fans of Northern Ireland by joining Celtic the previous year, when his family in Lurgan had also received threats.

Dennis Wise (December 2002) – The Millwall midfielder was sent a number of death-threat letters after taking former club Leicester to court over £2.3m of lost earnings. Wise was sacked for allegedly punching team-mate Callum Davidson on a pre-season tour.

Robbie Savage (March 2003) – Birmingham midfielder Savage had death threats sent to his own website after his involvement in a stormy derby clash against Aston Villa.

HIT WHERE IT HURTS
Nobody likes a cheat, so when the clubs try to break the rules and get caught they can expect the Football Association to come down hard.

Points deductions are still pretty rare, so the FA's main punishment is to hit the clubs in the wallet with big fines. Here are some of the heaviest ...

£1,500,000: Tottenham were fined £600,000 and docked 12 points in 1994 for financial irregularities involving loans to players. On appeal, the points deduction was cut to six, but the fine was increased to £1.5m.

£175,000: Arsenal had to stump up a huge amount after being found guilty of failing to control their players in a controversial goalless draw against Manchester United at Old Trafford in 2003.

£150,000: Leeds and Tottenham were both fined this amount in 2000 for a mass players' brawl at Elland Road.

£105,000: Chelsea were punished in 1991 for making illegal payments to players.

£100,000: League newcomers Boston United were fined in 2002 – and also had four points deducted – for financial irregularities involving contracts.

£90,000: Tottenham were punished by UEFA in 1996 for fielding a weakened team in the Intertoto Cup.

£75,000: Chelsea were fined in 1988 following serious crowd trouble at a play-off match against Middlesbrough.

£75,000: Everton were found guilty in 1994 of 'poaching' manager Mike Walker from Norwich City.

£60,000: Wimbledon were ordered by UEFA in 1996 to fork out for fielding a weakened team in the Intertoto Cup.

£55,000: Birmingham were fined in 1994 for 'poaching' manager Barry Fry from Southend.

FANTASTIC FOOTBALL FACTS

PLAY IT AGAIN, SAM
Replays are a vital part of cup football – designed to finally separate the teams after a drawn match.

But, with football being a 'funny old game', there can be some weird and wonderful occasions when winning sides are forced to give their opponents another bite at the cherry ...

15 December 1999: West Ham v Aston Villa (Worthington Cup quarter-final) – West Ham thought they'd won 5–4 on penalties but substitute Emmanuel Omoyinmi, on for the final six minutes of extra time, was cup-tied having already played in the competition while on loan at Gillingham. The Football League ordered a replay which the Hammers promptly lost 3–1.

27 September 1999: Herne Bay v Farnham (FA Cup second qualifying round) – Herne Bay used four replacements instead of three during their 2–1 win. The FA ordered a replay but Herne Bay again won 2–1.

13 February 1999: Arsenal v Sheffield United (FA Cup fifth round) – Arsenal's Ray Parlour threw the ball back towards United keeper Alan Kelly after the Sheffield player had kicked it into touch so teammate Lee Morris could get treatment. But Parlour's throw was intercepted by Nwankwo Kanu who crossed the ball and Marc Overmars scored the 'winner' for a 2–1 victory. Arsene Wenger offered to replay the match and the FA agreed. Arsenal again won 2–1.

25 November 1992: Peterborough v Kingstonian (FA Cup first round) – Peterborough hammered the minnows 9–1 but the FA ordered a replay after the Kingstonian goalkeeper was hit by a missile. Peterborough squeezed past the non-League side 1–0 in the replay.

5 January 1985: Leicester v Burton Albion (FA Cup third round) – Leicester beat the non-League side 6–1 but the FA ordered a replay behind closed doors after the Burton goalkeeper suffered concussion when he was hit by a coin thrown from the crowd. The rematch was played at Coventry and Leicester scraped through 1–0.

March 1974: Newcastle v Nottingham Forest (FA Cup sixth round) – The FA intervened after the crowd invaded the pitch in an attempt to get the match abandoned with Forest leading 3–1. The game continued and Newcastle fought back to win 4–3 but the FA ordered a replay because of the crowd interference. Newcastle won at Goodison Park 1–0.

October 1887: Everton v Bolton. (FA Cup first round) – Bolton won 1–0 but the match was ruled void because they used an ineligible player. In farcical circumstances Everton won the replay but were themselves disqualified for using two barred players.

READ THE SMALL PRINT
Clubs will move heaven and earth to get the right player, although sometimes they are virtually held to ransom by the pampered stars in order to finally persuade them to sign on the dotted line.

Here are a selection of top names who knew exactly what they wanted when they joined their new team, although sometimes the clubs can be strong enough to put their foot down ...

Edmundo
The Brazilian had a clause in his contract with Fiorentina letting him go to the Rio carnival. He also demanded a four-wheel Cherokee Jeep – which he duly crashed – and looked at 100 houses before settling on a castle.

Jürgen Klinsmann
In his first spell at Tottenham, Jürgen the German demanded a 'happy' clause in his contract that meant if, for any reason, he was

FANTASTIC FOOTBALL FACTS

unhappy at White Hart Lane he could quit the club. In his second spell with Spurs, he negotiated a clause which ensured he was guaranteed a place in the side if he was fit.

Stefan Schwarz
The Sunderland midfielder had booked himself on the first passenger flight to the moon, but manager Peter Reid told him to forget his lunar ambitions if he wanted to join the club.

Attilio Lombardo
The bald Italian demanded a Surrey mansion with a butler and maid to look after him as a condition of his transfer from Sampdoria to Crystal Palace. The Eagles told Lombardo to forget it, but he still moved to Selhurst Park.

Ian Wright
Motorbike fanatic Wright was banned by Arsenal from riding his beloved Harley Davidson.

Fabrizio Ravanelli
The White Feather's proposed move to Everton in 2000 fell through when he demanded 28 free first-class flights to Italy from Merseyside on top of his £200,000 signing-on fee.

Andy Goram
Goram, who represented Scotland at cricket, was banned by Rangers from playing the summer game in case he injured his hands.

Carlos Roa
The former Argentinian national goalkeeper stunned Real Mallorca in 1999 by walking out on the club because he was convinced the world was going to end on the first day of the new Millennium.

SMALLEST ENGLAND PLAYERS

They say that football is a physical game and there are many instances of players who have failed to make the grade after being labelled 'too small'. However, that didn't stop these little fellas making their mark and representing England.

Fanny Walden (2 caps, 1914–22) 5ft 2in

Danny Wallace (1 cap, 1986) 5ft 4in

Steve Coppell (42 caps, 1978–83) 5ft 5in

Nick Barmby (23 caps, 1995–2002) 5ft 6in

Dennis Wise (21 caps, 1991–2001) 5ft 6in

Joe Cole (15 caps, 2001–2004) 5ft 7in

Paul Scholes (60 caps, 1997–2004) 5ft 7in

Paul Parker (19 caps, 1989–1994) 5ft 7in

Kenny Sansom (86 caps, 1979–1988) 5ft 7in

Alan Ball (72 caps, 1965–1975) 5ft 7in 72 caps

Darius Vassell (16 caps, 2002–2004) 5ft 7in

Stanley Matthews (54 caps, 1935–1957) 5ft 7in

SUSPENDED IN TIME

Do the crime and you have to serve the time. These players were left kicking their heels on the sidelines after falling foul of the authorities ...

Willie Woodburn (Rangers, 1954)

Banned for life after being sent off three times for retaliation between March 1953 and August 1954. The ban was rescinded three years later but Woodburn had already retired by then.

191

FANTASTIC FOOTBALL FACTS

Billy Cook (Oldham, 1915)
Received a 12-month ban for refusing to leave the field after he was dismissed when playing at Middlesbrough. The match had to be abandoned with 35 minutes to go.

Billy McLafferty (Stenhousemuir, 1992)
Banned for eight-and-a-half-months for failing to turn up at a Scottish FA hearing after he was sent off against Arbroath.

Eric Cantona (Manchester United, 1995)
Banned for eight months and fined £10,000 by the Football Association for attacking a spectator after being sent off against Crystal Palace.

Rio Ferdinand (Manchester United, 2003)
The England defender was forced to miss eight months of action, including the Euro 2004 tournament, after failing to turn up for a drugs test after training at Manchester United.

Frank Barson (Watford, 1928)
Banned for seven months after being sent off against Fulham.

Duncan Ferguson (Everton, 1995)
SFA suspended him for 12 matches for violent conduct when playing for Rangers against Raith. A Scottish judge quashed seven games of the ban.

Paolo Di Canio (Sheffield Wednesday, 1998)
Received an 11-match ban from the Football Association, including a statutory three matches for being sent off during the home match against Arsenal, after which he shoved referee Paul Alcock to the ground. He was also fined £10,000.

Paul Davis (Arsenal, 1988)
Suspended for nine matches and fined a then-record £3,000 for breaking the jaw of Glenn Cockerill.

Frank Sinclair (Chelsea/West Brom, 1992)
Nine-match ban and £600 fine after being found guilty of assaulting referee Paul Alcock when on loan to West Brom.

Mark Dennis (Queens Park Rangers, 1987)
Sent off 11 times in his career and answered two disrepute charges concerning newspaper articles. Suspended for 53 days; amended on appeal to eight games.

Alan Gough (Gillingham, 1993)
Goalkeeper who was suspended for 42 days after assaulting a referee.

Dean Windass (Aberdeen, 1997)
The striker was effectively sent off three times in the opening half of their 5–0 defeat at Dundee United. The SFA gave him a six-match ban after being dismissed for two bookable offences, abusing the referee and ripping a corner flag up and throwing it into the ground on his way off.

Patrick Vieira (Arsenal, 1999)
The Arsenal midfielder was fined £45,000 and received a six-match ban from the FA for spitting at West Ham defender Neil Ruddock after being sent off in a Premiership clash at Upton Park.

Roy Keane (Manchester United, 2002)
The Republic of Ireland hardman was suspended for five matches and handed a £150,000 fine for bringing the game into disrepute for a claim in his autobiography that he deliberately set out to hurt Manchester City midfielder Alf Inge Haaland in a game in April 2001.

FANTASTIC FOOTBALL FACTS

THE NAME GAME
Ever wished that Bobby or Jack Charlton had actually turned out for Charlton? Or perhaps you are a Darlington fan that wants your club to sign Jermaine Darlington. Some players seem to be perfectly named to play for certain clubs and every so often the dream becomes reality. Here are a selection ...

Charlie Aston (Aston Villa), 1897–1900

Ben Barnett (Barnet), 1993

Dave Barnett (Barnet), 1991–1993

Arthur Blackburn (Blackburn Rovers), 1899–1901

Fred Blackburn (Blackburn Rovers), 1897–1904

R Bolton (Bolton Wanderers), 1898

Lew Bradford (Bradford City), 1946–1948

F Burton (Burton Swifts), 1898–1900

Alf Berry (Bury), 1905

John Berry (Bury), 1897–1902

Norman Berry (Bury), 1945–1947

Andy Lincoln (Lincoln City), 1931

Sidney Swinden (Swindon Town), 1937–1938

WEMBLEY LOWS
Wembley evokes feelings for football fans around the world and has long been rated as one of the top stadiums by the players themselves.

FA Cup finals, European Cup finals and even that famous World Cup final have graced the hallowed turf, but Wembley is most famous for being the home of the England team.

However, that does not mean that supporters were blindly obsessed as these shockingly low Wembley attendances down the years prove:

15,628: England v Chile (Friendly), May 1989

20,038: England v Colombia (Friendly), September 1995

21,142: England v Japan (Umbro Cup), June 1995

21,342: England v Czechoslovakia (Friendly), April 1990

23,789: England v USSR (Friendly), May 1991

23,951: England v East Germany (Friendly), September 1984

25,756: England v Colombia (Rous Cup), May 1988

25,837: England v Denmark (Friendly), September 1988

27,643: England v Denmark (Friendly), May 1990

28,592: England v Portugal (Friendly), December 1995

STRANGE BUT TRUE

We've tried to cover every weird and wonderful angle of the beautiful game in this book, but some facts are so strange that they defy categorisation. Here are the bizarre tales that you just could not make up . . .

India qualified for the World Cup Finals for the first time in 1950. But they withdrew when they were refused permission to play in bare feet.

When Coventry defeated Aldershot 7–1 in a Fourth Division match in November 1958, they set a record for the biggest Football League win with an understrength team. The Sky Blues had lost goalkeeper Jim Sanders with a broken leg and substitutes were not then permitted.

A French flag could not be found when France faced Romania in Newcastle during Euro '96. Organisers turned a Dutch flag on its end but spectators spotted that it was the wrong shape.

Ecuadorian player Ataulfo Valencia was sent off for lashing out at the driver of an injury cart after being run over by him during a Libertadores Cup match.

The Portuguese Football Federation banned Bolivian Erwin Sanchez for six months after he tested positive for coke. Sanchez admitted the offence – he had drunk a can of Coca-Cola containing the prohibited substance caffeine.

During the 1928–29 season Halifax Town fielded two fortysomethings in goal. When regular Howard Matthews, a 44-year-old

FANTASTIC FOOTBALL FACTS

Welshman, and reserve Cliff Binns were injured, trainer Bob Suter, three months short of his 50th birthday, volunteered to play in goal. Suter had made his League debut for Notts County 28 years earlier and had not played in the competition for seven years until facing South Shields and Darlington in Division Three North matches four days apart. Both were lost 2–0.

Liverpool's staff between the world wars had a decidedly cosmopolitan look. On the Anfield books were: Elisha Scott (an Irishman), Robert Ireland (Scottish), Sam English (Irish) and George Poland (Welsh). Don Welsh (English) managed the club after the Second World War.

Leeds United once offered a trial to a talented youngster known as Del to club scouts. Embarrassed Elland Road officials called it off when they discovered Del was a 12–year-old schoolGIRL.

When the USA trainer ran on to attend an injured player during the 1930 World Cup Finals he tripped, fell and broke a bottle of chloroform in his bag. He had to be carried off unconscious while the player recovered without treatment.

After scoring two own goals at Mansfield in 1982, Bristol City defender Rob Newman returned to the dressing room in tears – to find his wallet had been stolen!

On Christmas Day 1937 dense fog caused the Charlton v Chelsea game to be abandoned after 61 minutes. When the Charlton players had been back in their dressing room almost ten minutes someone spotted that legendary goalkeeper Sam Bartram was missing. Bartram was found still in his goalmouth peering into the gloom for oncoming forwards!

A pre-match praying ritual for the goalkeeper with Brazilian club Rio Preto was rudely interrupted when opponents Corinthians scored after three seconds while he was still on his knees.

In 1988 Hearts director Douglas Park was so incensed with the decisions of referee David Symes in a match with Rangers that he locked the official in the dressing rooms and marched off with the key.

Dublin City had an application to join the Scottish League rejected in 1990.

When striker Duncan Ferguson joined Everton he had a clause inserted in his contract stating that he must have a house with a pigeon loft.

Birmingham defender Liam Daish was once out of tune with referees. When a supporter threw a trumpet on the pitch during a match against Chester, Daish picked it up and began playing it. The referee sent him off for ungentlemanly conduct.

Former League club Workington increased their board of directors to 13 in 1966. At that stage they had more directors than full-time players.

In 1911 a local butcher donated a sheep to the first Morton player who scored. Striker Tom Gracie won a lamb called Toby who became the club's mascot. But Toby was left in the dressing room when the team went to the pub – and drowned in the bath.

Peter Knowles unexpectedly quit Wolves and football in 1969 to become a full-time Jehovah's Witness. But not before settling a £7 10s bill from Portsmouth for replacing a ball he kicked out of their Fratton Park ground in celebration of a goal he scored there.